The
THE BIBLE BIBLE

First Church of the
BRETHREN
CARLISLE, PA-

DISCOVERING THE BIBLE

DISCOVERING
THE BIBLE

G. W. H. Lampe
and David Scott Daniell

illustrations by
Steele Savage

Nashville   **ABINGDON PRESS**   **New York**

The authors and publishers wish to express their appreciation to the following
for the use of photographs: The Trustees of the British Museum for the pictures
facing pages 90, 100, 111, 127, 129; Wide World Photos, Inc. for picture facing
page 92; The Master and Fellows of Trinity College, Cambridge, for the picture
facing page 98; and the Reverend Canon C. E. Matthews for the picture facing
page 114.

Scripture quotations unless otherwise noted, are from the Revised Standard
Version of the Bible, copyright © 1946 and © 1952 by the Division of Christian
Education, National Council of Churches, and are used by permission.

The quotation on page 123 is from The New English Bible, New Testament.
© The Delegates of the Oxford University Press and The Syndics of the Cambridge University Press 1961. Reprinted by permission.

Discovering the Bible was first issued in Great Britain by University of London
Press, Ltd., copyright © 1961 by David Scott Daniell and G. W. H. Lampe.

FOREWORD

The Bible is a very important book. The way of life of the European and American peoples is based on its teachings. Christians look to the Bible for guidance and its message has strengthened their faith for nearly two thousand years.

As the authors of this book say, the best way to get to know the Bible is to read it, and to read it again until its inspiration stays in our memory. It contains some of the best stories there are—stories of Old Testament heroes and the stories of Christ. This book will not tell the stories for you, but it will help you to find them, for it is sometimes difficult to find your way about among all the books which compose the Bible.

The Bible is a very old book, and it has been translated very many times. The stories in the first part of this book tell you how the life and teaching of Jesus came to be written down, how Paul wrote his letters, and how learned men tried to decide which was the correct form of the many versions which were written.

The story of how the Bible came to be translated into English, the difficulties and dangers encountered by the men who were prepared to risk their lives to do this, make vivid reading.

If *Discovering the Bible* helps you to understand your Bible better, and makes you appreciate it because so many people have worked and suffered to preserve it for you; if it encourages you to read some of the books mentioned in the book list, about life in the land of the Bible and about the life of Jesus and his people, it will have served its purpose.

> ALYS L. GREGORY, Editor of the
> *Discovery Reference Books* for
> the University of London Press, Ltd.

CONTENTS

PART I
Stories About the Bible

PART II
Reference Section

PART III
The Bible

PART I

Stories About the Bible

Long ago, in the days when only a few could read and write, people told stories both to entertain and to inform. They reported to each other news they had heard.

All the information and all the stories which today we may read in the Bible were first told by word of mouth. Later wise men and scholars recorded the various happenings and the stories, but sometimes hundreds of years had passed before the writing took place. Two different people would write the story in slightly different ways. Often several people wrote an account of the same happening or story.

The stories and happenings of the Old Testament were recorded in the Hebrew language; the New Testament in Greek. No doubt the writers themselves were very different. Some may have been young, some old. Some may have lived in cities, some in small villages. Each presented the story as he understood it, in the language most familiar to him.

The study of the Bible has held the attention of scholars and of devoted men and women through the centuries. Countless people have spent their whole lives interpreting its writings.

> The stories which follow in Part I of this book have been made up. Though all are based in part on fact or tradition, some of the characters and some of the incidents are purely imaginary. It is hoped these stories will lead you to investigate the Bible for yourself.

CHAPTER I

The Best Story in the World

Our story begins about nineteen hundred years ago, on a bright morning in the year A.D. 64, when two young men met in a street in Rome. Their names were Severus and Gallus.

"Good day to you, Gallus my friend," Severus said. "Why is there such a crowd up there by the Forum?"

"It's because of the lions, Severus. They've stopped the wagons so that the people can look at them. They're bringing them to the arena for tomorrow's games. They're magnificent beasts."

The two young men thought about the games for a moment. Thousands of excited Romans would be packed on the tiers of stone seats. The Emperor would be there in full state. The gate at the bottom of the arena wall would be raised and the lions would slink out and stand blinking in the sun, flicking their tails from side to side and snarling. Then they would get the scent of the little group of victims and start to walk towards them, lifting their heads to roar.

At that moment one of the lions in the wagon roared. The majestic noise echoed down the street and Severus shuddered.

"What poor wretches are to be sacrificed to the lions tomorrow?" he asked.

"Oh, no one important. I'm afraid it will be but poor sport. It's only some of these people they call

Christians. There's no fight in them, they're a cowardly lot. All they do is stand there, praying and singing hymns."

Severus looked at his friend with surprise. "Cowardly?" he said. "Do you think that is cowardly? Why, as they wait for the lions to pounce they actually look happy in the face of death! I've never seen anything like it! It's wonderful."

"What's this, Severus?" said Gallus, looking sharply at his friend. "You, an educated, well-born Roman, speaking well of these Christians! Why, they're a danger to the state!"

"How can such poor people be dangerous to the state?" Severus asked.

"Because they have dangerous ideas! They say a slave is as good as we are! They despise riches. And they deny the gods of Rome."

"They've got a God of their own," said Severus, "called Jesus Christ."

"Oh, yes, and I'll tell you who He was. He was a common Jewish carpenter who was crucified in Jerusalem as a criminal about thirty years ago! Yet these madmen say He was the Son of God! They say He was the saviour of the world. No, the Emperor is quite right: they must be destroyed. But talking of Christians, Severus, do you see that man coming toward us?"

"With the look of a scholar?"

"Yes. His name's Mark. I met him the other day

12

and I think he's one of those Christians. I'll tease him! We'll have some fun! You watch me."

"Oh, leave him alone," said Severus.

Gallus hailed the young man.

"Well, Mark," he said, "have you been looking at the lions?"

Mark stopped. "No," he said, "I passed by."

"That was a pity," said Gallus. "They are going to devour some Christians in the arena tomorrow. I'm going to watch. Are you?"

"No, I shall not go," said Mark.

"Oh, I see," Gallus said. "But you agree it's a just fate for the followers of this Jesus of Nazareth, eh?"

Mark looked away and said something under his breath. Severus, feeling sorry for such a gentle man, wanted to say something friendly. "I'm not going either," he said, "but Gallus enjoys watching helpless men and women being torn to pieces by starving lions."

"And so do all true Romans," said Gallus. "Tell me, Mark, are you not a Christian yourself?"

Mark looked at Gallus and then at Severus, but he said nothing.

"Come, my friend," said Gallus again. "Answer me! Do you believe that Jesus of Nazareth is 'the Son of God'? Would you be prepared to face the lions for your belief? Well?"

"Oh, let him be," said Severus. "It is none of your business."

"Oh, but it is my business!" said Gallus. "It is our duty to the Emperor to denounce Christians. That is why I am asking him. Well Mark, for the third time, are you a Christian or not?"

"No, of course not," Mark blurted out. "Of course I am not a Christian." He hurried away, pushing through the throng of people in the street. Severus noticed his anguished look. But Gallus laughed. "Truly he is no Christian after all, for they never deny their faith, even when it means death!"

Mark went to a house and knocked at the door. He was admitted, and went through to a small walled garden at the back where an old man was dozing in the shade of a fig tree.

"Peter," he said, "it is I, Mark."

The old man opened his eyes. "Welcome, Mark," he said. "The peace of our Lord be with you."

"And with you, too, Peter."

"But what is amiss?" said the old man. "You are troubled."

"I have done a dreadful thing," said Mark, "I have —I have denied our Lord."

The old man looked up sharply. "You have denied our Lord? Then tell me about it," he said kindly.

"As I was coming here," said Mark, "I saw the lions being taken to the amphitheatre. Some of our brethren are to die tomorrow, in the arena."

"I know it," the old man said. "May the Lord give

them the strength to endure. But what happened when you saw the lions?"

"I met two Roman citizens. One of them, a lawyer named Gallus, taunted me with being a Christian, and asked me directly whether I was or not. I had not the courage to declare my faith! I denied Our Lord."

"Sit down here by me," said the old man gently. "I have something to tell you. Ah—did you hear that?"

"I only heard a cock crow," said Mark as he sat down.

"Yes, a cock crowed. A cock crowed also when I denied Our Lord!"

"When you denied Jesus?" said Mark. "But that could not be! You, the chief of the Apostles?"

"Listen, and I will tell you. It was on the evening before He was crucified. We all supped together in Jerusalem, Jesus and all of us twelve disciples. I remember that Jesus was sorrowful that night. Afterwards we went to the Mount of Olives, outside the city, and He told us that His hour of suffering was at hand."

"So He knew what would happen?" Mark asked.

"Yes, He knew. He knew also that we would all desert Him when He needed us most. Oh, we denied it, of course! I said, 'Even though they all fall away, I will not.' "

"And what did Jesus say?" Mark asked.

The old man did not answer for a moment or two. His thoughts were far away in a garden outside the walls of Jerusalem, more than thirty years before. After a while, he turned to Mark and went on. "Jesus said to me, 'Truly I say to you, Peter, this very night before the cock crows twice, you will deny me three times.'"

"Go on," said Mark, absorbed in the story.

"Then we all went into a garden outside the city. It was called Gethsemane. He went a little way apart to pray and told three of us to keep watch. But we fell asleep. Suddenly an angry crowd of people came with swords and staves seeking Jesus. Judas Iscariot was with them, and he went up to Jesus and kissed Him. It was the sign he had arranged to betray Jesus to the Chief Priests. The mob rushed at Jesus, jeering and shouting; they mocked Him and they beat Him."

"But," said Mark, "what did you do?"

"What did we do?" said the old man with a sigh. "Why, we ran away! We, the disciples He loved and trusted, we ran away."

Again the old man fell silent, and Mark did not dare to break into his sad thoughts. "There is more," Peter said. "I must tell you all. When they took Jesus to the Palace of the High Priest I followed and waited in an outer room, with the servants. I was sitting in the doorway when a serving maid came up to me and said: 'You also were with the Nazarene, Jesus.' I was frightened, and I said I didn't know what she meant. I went out onto the porch—and a cock crowed!"

"As Jesus had prophesied," Mark said.

"Yes, as the Master had said. I stood there on the

porch looking out, and someone else saw me and said I was one of the disciples, and again I denied it. Then someone came up and peered into my face. 'Certainly you are one of them; for you are a Galilean.' And I became angry and said, 'I do not know this man of whom you speak.' At that very moment a cock crowed again. Then did I remember what Jesus had said, and I went into the garden and I wept."

"So you see," said Peter after another silence, "my denial of Our Lord was far worse than yours. Yet He forgave me. He will forgive you."

"Do you really think so?" Mark asked.

"I am sure of it. Your time is not yet."

After a while Mark said: "There is another thing which troubles me."

"What is that?"

"How will men know the true story of Our Lord when you are dead? You knew him in life, and heard Him teach."

"Those to whom I have told the story, and those to whom the other disciples told it, will tell others, and so it will spread."

"Yet, Peter, the memory of man is short. Some things will be forgotten. Others will be invented, and the truth will be lost."

"I know what is in your mind, Mark. Yes, men must have these things always in remembrance. Otherwise men will follow cunningly devised fables and Our Lord will be forgotten. That must never be. I will tell you what I saw and heard. I will tell you what Jesus did and what He taught us, how He died on the cross and was dead and buried, and rose again, and ascended into heaven."

"Tell me now, Peter," Mark said eagerly.

And Peter began: "Passing along by the Sea of Galilee, Jesus saw Andrew, my brother, and me casting a net in the sea, for we were fishermen. And Jesus said to us, 'Follow me and I will make you fishers of men.' And immediately we left our nets and followed him."

Peter, who had been one of the closest friends of Jesus, told the story in his gentle voice. You can read it for yourself in the Gospel According to Mark, the most wonderful story in the world.

The Gospel which Mark wrote nineteen hundred years ago was copied again and again, and then the copies were copied again and again and read by the new Christians. Three other stories of the life and teaching of Jesus were written—the Gospels of Matthew, Luke, and John.

Note: There was a tradition about A.D. 140 that Mark, who was Peter's interpreter, did indeed write down all that Peter told him about Jesus. In the third century it was reported that Mark wrote his Gospel while Peter was alive. Another writer has said he wrote after Peter's death. There are other traditions, and we can not be sure about it.

19

CHAPTER II

The Letters of Paul

The Gospels tell us that after Jesus was crucified and buried He rose from the dead and appeared to His disciples. He gave them a command. "Go therefore," he said, "and make disciples of all nations, baptizing them in the name of the Father and of the Son and of the Holy Spirit, teaching them to observe all that I have commanded you; and lo, I am with you always, to the close of the age." (Matt. 28:19-20.)

So the disciples set forth and traveled throughout the countries around the Mediterranean Sea, which represented the known world to the Jews of those days. As they journeyed they told people about Jesus and about His teaching. The men, women, and children who wanted to become followers of Jesus Christ were baptized and became *Christians*. When a number of people had been baptized the disciples formed a church in the town where they were preaching.

The word "church" does not only mean a building with a tower or spire. Its first meaning was the community of Christians. Each community of Christians was also called a "church." It was through these earliest churches that Christianity was to spread, and you can read the story in the Acts of the Apostles. The hero of the later chapters of Acts is Paul.

Paul was a very unusual man. Originally his name was Saul. He was a well-to-do Jew born in Tarsus in

Asia Minor. Shortly after Jesus was crucified, Saul was living in Jerusalem, studying Jewish law. The Jews hated the Christians bitterly, and Saul became their leader, hunting Christians to throw them into prison.

Then a wonderful thing happened. One day, when Saul was traveling from Jerusalem to Damascus, seeking out Christians to punish them, he suddenly saw a bright light. It was so vivid that he was struck blind and remained blind for three days. From the light came a voice which said, "Saul, Saul, why do you persecute me?" Saul knew it was the voice of Jesus, rebuking him because he did not recognize Jesus as the Messiah, the Son of God. From that moment he was changed. Saul, the enemy the Christians feared most, became Paul, their bravest and most devoted leader, who spent the rest of his life working for the Christian faith.

Paul traveled far and wide, preaching Christianity and organizing churches throughout the western world. He often wrote letters to the new churches he founded. They are powerful, manly letters; some of them have been preserved, and from them we know about the beginnings of the Christian Church. You can read these letters in the New Testament, where they are placed after the Acts of the Apostles. They are called the Letters of Paul.

What was he like, this great man who lived nineteen hundred years ago, and who still speaks to us in his letters? It is said that he was rather an ungainly man with a gruff voice. He was certainly a great leader and brave as a lion.

Some thirty years after Paul's conversion, he was in Rome, and a young man named Tychicus went to see him. Tychicus had to make quite a long journey because he lived in Ephesus, a town near the west coast of the country now known as Turkey.

When Tychicus arrived in Rome he found that Paul was in prison. He got permission to see him and was taken to the cell. Paul was sitting at a little table near the tiny window, reading a parchment which he held close to his eyes.

"The peace of God be with you," said Tychicus. "It is I, Tychicus from Ephesus."

Paul put down his parchment and came across the cell, his hands outstretched.

"Why, Tychicus, my son, you are welcome indeed. You bring news of the brethren at Ephesus and of Timothy?"

"I bring a letter from Timothy, the head of our church at Ephesus. He begs you to go to see him, for we need you in our church."

"I would gladly go to Ephesus," said Paul, "but as you see, I am in prison."

"But perhaps they will soon set you free!"

"Nay, Tychicus," said Paul, "I am soon to stand my trial and I know the sentence will be—death!"

"It cannot be," said Tychicus in horror.

Paul nodded and smiled. "I am ready to be offered," he said. "The time of my departure has come. I have fought a good fight. I have finished the race, I have kept the faith!"

He began to pace slowly up and down the dark prison cell.

"I have suffered more than most," said Paul, "with far greater labors, far more imprisonments, with countless beatings, and often near death. Five times I have received at the hands of the Jews the forty lashes less one. Three times I have been beaten with rods; once I was stoned. Three times I have been shipwrecked; a night and a day have been adrift at sea; on frequent journeys, in danger from rivers, danger from robbers, danger from my own people, danger from Gentiles, danger in the city, danger in the wilderness, danger at sea, danger from false brethren; in toil and hardship, through many a sleepless night, in hunger and thirst, often without food, in cold and exposure. And, apart from other things, there is the daily pressure upon me of my anxiety for all the churches."

Paul stopped and turned to Tychicus. "Once in Damascus the governor kept the city under guard, hoping to seize me, but I was let down in a basket through a window in the wall and escaped. But this time there will be no escape, nor do I desire it, for I am ready."

"But, Paul," said Tychicus, "what will happen to the churches without you to guide us?"

"Have no fear, my son. The churches will live. Christ's teaching will be spread throughout the whole world. There will always be some to show the power and the love of our Lord. But I would that Timothy should come here to see me, before it is too late."

"I will tell him to come."

"I want him to bring my cloak which I left when I was last at Ephesus, and my books and the parchments that are there, for I must write letters to all the brethren in all the churches."

Paul went to the window and read the letter which Tychicus had brought. When he had finished he said: "Sit down at the table, my son, take a reed and write this letter."

Tychicus got ready and Paul waited, glancing at the letter from Timothy. Then he said, "Write this, my son. 'Paul an apostle of Christ Jesus by the will of God, according to the promise of life which is in Christ Jesus. To Timothy, my beloved child: Grace, Mercy and Peace, from God the Father and Christ Jesus our Lord. . . .' "

So Tychicus wrote the letter, and you can read it in your Bible. It is called the Second Letter of Paul to Timothy. Toward the end of the letter you will see that Paul does ask Timothy to bring him his cloak, his books, and the parchments. He also warns Timothy against a coppersmith, named Alexander, who is a dangerous enemy to the Christians in Ephesus.

You can read Paul's words, when he is describing his life and his sufferings, in the Second Letter of Paul to the Corinthians (11:23-33).

The early Christians treasured these letters. They copied them many times, and they read them in their services. Thirteen of them have come down to us, and we can read them in the Bible today, nineteen hundred years later.

The four Gospels, the Acts of the Apostles, Paul's letters, letters from other Apostles, and the Book of Revelation make up the New Testament, the book on which Christianity is founded. It is believed they were all written within one hundred years after the death of Jesus. We are not sure of the order in which they were written, but we know that Paul's letters were written before the Gospels.

> Some of the books which are described traditionally as "Letters from Paul" (and are so designated in the Bibles we read today) are believed to have been written after Paul's time. Many think the letters to Timothy and Titus were written after Paul's death by someone who was trying to show what Paul would have advised young ministers of that time.

CHAPTER III

Buried Treasure

A farmer and his son were plowing a stony field near Jericho in Palestine over seventeen hundred years ago. The ox tugged the plow, the boy Joachim tried manfully to keep the furrows straight. Joachim's father led the ox. Suddenly Joachim shouted to the ox, which stopped pulling, and his father turned to see what had happened. Joachim was kneeling down to examine something in the newly plowed ground.

"Look, Father, the plow has struck something in the ground!" Joachim said excitedly. "It looks like the top of an earthenware jar!"

"A jar, buried in the ground?" said his father. "I have heard of such. Perhaps it is gold! Quick, dig it out."

Together they dug away the earth with their hands.

"How could there be gold buried in a jar in the ground?" Joachim asked.

"They say that once a temple stood here. It was destroyed, but the treasure might have been hidden."

"It is buried deep, Father."

"They bury gold deep, my son. Ah, if it is gold I shall buy another ox, for this one is old and lazy. You shall have new red sandals, my son, and we shall have two slaves. Now, up with it! If it is full of gold it will be heavy."

But the jar was not heavy.

"Throw it away," said Joachim's father in disgust.

"There's no gold. And the top is broken and there is a hole in the side. It's quite useless. Come, back to the plow."

"But, Father, there *is* something inside," said Joachim. "Look! A thick roll of papyrus, covered with writing."

"Papyrus? You can't eat papyrus! And what is the good of all that old writing? Throw it away, boy."

But Joachim was looking at the faded yellow roll.

"Father," he said earnestly, "please let me take this roll to the wise man at Caesarea. Please!"

"Take that rotten old roll to Caesarea, sixty miles away? Whatever for?"

"A little while ago, Father, a traveler came to the village. He said that a learned scholar named Origen at Caesarea has asked everyone to take him any old writings they find. They are sometimes very valuable."

"Valuable, old writing? Nonsense!"

"They say he pays money for them, Father."

"Then surely he must be mad! But if he pays money . . . well, perhaps you can go."

"Oh, thank you Father, thank you," said Joachim. He put the writings back in the jar, put it in the shade, and took up the plow again.

A few days later he set off for Caesarea, on the coast of Palestine. He wrapped the precious roll in cloth and stepped out briskly along the winding dusty tracks. At Caesarea he washed in a stream, combed his hair, and asked where he could find the scholar Origen. He was directed to a building in a narrow shady street. Inside, he went into a large room, where he looked round him with wonder.

The walls were lined with pigeon-holes, in which were hundreds and hundreds of rolls of papyrus similar to his, while larger ones stood in baskets on the floor. Colored tabs were attached to them. In the center of the room a dozen men stood at desks; reading, copying, or examining ancient rolls, some of skin and some of papyrus. For a country boy who could not read or write, but who longed to be a scholar, it was a wonderful sight.

Soon a young man asked Joachim what he wanted. Joachim put his parcel on the table and carefully unwrapped the roll of papyrus. "Please, sir," he said, "when my father and I were plowing our fields we struck a jar buried in the ground and inside it was this!"

"Buried in the ground in a jar, eh?" said the young man, looking at the writing. "Where was this?"

"Near Jericho, sir. I had heard that Master Origen wanted all such ancient writings, so I have brought it."

The young man did not say anything. He was absorbed in examining the Hebrew writing on the roll, which he unwound carefully.

"Please, sir," said Joachim, "will Master Origen want it?"

"I can't say for sure," said the young man, "but I believe it is a very old copy of the Book of Ecclesiastes.

Master Origen will know. If it is, then you have done very well, and he will assuredly reward you."

"Please, sir," said Joachim, "why does Master Origen want these old writings?"

"Ah, that's a big question, my young friend. I'll tell you. Master Origen used to be a great teacher in Alexandria in Egypt. He is a Christian, and one day he determined to devote his life and his learning to one tremendous task, to revise and write out the Greek version of the ancient Jewish Scriptures. He left Alexandria and came here to Caesarea in Palestine."

"But, sir, if he is a Christian, why does he want to write out the ancient Jewish Scriptures?"

The young man looked at Joachim and nodded his head approvingly. "My young friend, you assuredly have an inquiring mind. And that is good. Why, you ask, do Christians, who follow the teachings of Jesus Christ as set down in the New Testament, want to read the Jewish Scriptures? Let me ask you a question. What people did Jesus belong to?"

"He was a Jew, sir."

"Exactly. So, of course, he was brought up on the Jewish Scriptures. Do you know the story of Jesus in the Temple?"

"I don't think so, sir."

"It was when He was about the same age as you—about twelve. His parents went from their home at Nazareth to Jerusalem, as all devout Jews did, for the

Feast of the Passover, and, of course, they took Jesus with them. When the time came for them to go home they couldn't find the boy Jesus. They hunted for Him for three days, and you can imagine how they worried."

"He was lost in Jerusalem?"

"Yes, and do you know where they found him?"

"No, sir."

"In the Temple. He was sitting with the learned priests asking them questions about the Scriptures. As boys of twelve often do," he added, with a smile. "But Jesus amazed them. Luke tells us in his Gospel that all who heard the boy were astonished at His understanding."

"And He was only twelve years old?" asked Joachim.

"Yes. So, you see, Jesus loved the old Jewish Scriptures, and He preached His new teaching from them, so Christians treasure them. And there is another reason: the books of the prophets foretell His coming on earth. That is why Christians read the books of the Jewish Scriptures, and read them just as they read the Gospels and the Letters of Paul and the rest of the New Testament. We call the old Scriptures the Old Testament. The Old Testament and the New fit together, they belong to each other. So that is why Master Origen is writing out the old Jewish Scriptures again in Greek.

"I see, sir," said Joachim. "But why does he write them in Greek? Are they not in Hebrew?"

"Because Greek is the language spoken by most Christians. The Old Testament was first translated from Hebrew into Greek very long ago, two hundred and fifty years before Jesus was born. That translation is called the Septuagint, which means the Seventy, because according to an ancient legend, the translation was made by seventy learned men."

"I see," said Joachim, wrinkling his nose as he thought hard. "But if the old Jewish Scriptures have already been translated from Hebrew into Greek, why is Master Origen doing it again?"

"Bless you, my boy, how you worry the bone to get all the meat off it!"

"I am sorry, sir."

"Nay, it is a splendid thing to ask questions to learn. You see, the Septuagint has been copied thousands of times, but no matter how careful a man is, when he copies very long books, of hundreds of pages, mistakes creep in. There are many reasons: the papyrus or skin on which it is written may be worn badly so that a word is blurred. The light may be poor, or the scholar may have bad eyesight. He may well miss out a whole line. Then, when that is copied, the mistakes are written again, and other mistakes are made. As the centuries pass, all the copies become different. Master Origen is trying to write a new and perfect version without mistakes."

"I think I understand now, sir," said Joachim. "And

so that he can make a perfect copy, he wants all the very old copies to compare them. And that is why he likes people to bring him old copies of the Scriptures when they find them."

"Exactly. Well done!"

Joachim looked round the room. "Sir," he asked, "are all these rolls in the pigeon-holes and baskets old books of the Scriptures?"

"Yes, and the colored tabs tell us which is which. Master Origen has a great knowledge of Hebrew and Greek and he can tell, by comparing different copies, which of many versions of the same passage is likely to be the true one. Come with me to that inner room, and I will show you some finished pages of the actual book he is writing."

The young man led Joachim to a small room. On a large table was a pile of parchment covered with columns of fine writing.

"This is the result of the master's work," the young man told Joachim. "He compares many different versions, and from studying them he decides what is the best. He dictates it to scribes, who write down the master's words in shorthand and then write it out like this. He has seven scribes who come in turn. As you see, the pages are ruled into six columns—see?"

"Yes, sir. Why is that?"

"The first column is the Jewish Scriptures in the Hebrew letters. The second column, this one, is the

same, with the words spelled out in Greek letters. The other four columns are the best versions he can find of other translations into Greek. This column, the fifth, is the translation I told you about, the Septuagint, which was made four hundred and fifty years ago."

"But, sir," said Joachim, "is he really writing out every book of the Old Testament six times?"

"Yes, all of it! It will take him twenty years or more. This is only one page of a thousand. The book is to be called the Hexapla, which means 'sixfold.' But look, here is Master Origen himself."

An·elderly man had come into the room, carrying a roll of parchment yellow with age. The young man went up to him.

"Master," said the young man, "here is a country boy from near Jericho who has brought a sacred roll he found buried in the ground."

Origen looked across at Joachim.

"My boy," he said, "I wish there were more like you in Palestine. So many precious writings are destroyed. What did he bring us, Eumenes?"

"This papyrus on the table, master. It may be an old version of Ecclesiastes."

"Ecclesiastes, eh? That would indeed be a treasure if it is in truth an old copy, for we have but few."

Origen went to the table and unrolled the ancient papyrus. He read in silence, a passage here, a passage there. Occasionally he looked closely at it, scrutinizing the Hebrew letters. Joachim watched him anxiously.

At last Origen straightened his back and looked at Joachim. "This is very important, my boy," he said. "I have not seen many rolls as old as this in such good condition."

"Then, sir," said Joachim, "will it help you in your work?"

"Indeed it will! Eumenes," he said to the young man, "listen to this. I translate it but roughly."

Origen began to read a passage from the papyrus. Joachim did not understand what it meant; but the lovely words and sentences enchanted him.

" 'Before the silver cord is snapped,' " Origen read, " 'or the golden bowl is broken, or the pitcher is broken at the fountain, or the wheel broken at the cistern, and the dust returns to the earth as it was, and the spirit returns to God who gave it. Vanity of Vanities, says the Preacher; all is vanity.' "

For a moment they were silent. Then Origen said, "What is your name, my boy?"

"Joachim, sir, the son of Jehudi."

"Well, Joachim, you shall be well rewarded, for you have brought me a great treasure."

"But, sir," said Joachim, "I want no money."

"Then what do you want, Joachim?" said Origen, looking at him with new interest.

Joachim hesitated. Then he summoned his courage and said: "Sir, I would like to work here, helping you."

"I see, can you read and write Hebrew and Greek?" asked Origen.

"No, sir, I cannot read or write. But I can learn!"

"Ah, that is well spoken! Listen, Joachim, return to Jericho with the money Eumenes will give you. Give it to your father and ask him for his blessing. Then return here to me."

"Master," said Joachim, hardly daring to believe his ears, "you mean I may work here for you?"

"You may. While you are studying and learning to read and write you can work labeling rolls, treating the old ones to preserve them as we shall show you, fetching and carrying. For I see that, untaught as you are, you have the heart of a true scholar."

"Oh, thank you, Master, thank you," said Joachim.

Note: On page 92 you may read more about the Septuagint, the first Greek translation of the Old Testament. The story of Jesus in the temple is found in Luke 2:40-52. The words which Master Origen read from the old roll of papyrus may be found in Eccl. 12:6-8. The story of Joachim and the jar he found has been made up. Origen, however, was a real person. He did write the six-column revision of the Old Testament, called the Hexapla, in Caesarea about A.D. 220. To help him in his work people took him old documents they found. As recently as 1947 a shepherd boy found some ancient scrolls hidden in a cave near the Dead Sea in Palestine. They had been there for nearly two thousand years. These are known as the Dead Sea Scrolls. Other fragments of ancient scrolls have been found since.

CHAPTER IV

Jerome the Hermit

One day in the year A.D. 382 a middle-aged priest, whose name was Father Jerome, was pacing restlessly up and down an anteroom in a palace in Rome. A young monk went to him.

"This way, please, Father," said the young monk.

The monk led the way down a splendid corridor and stood aside to allow Jerome to enter a room where an elderly bishop in a silk robe sat at a desk.

"The peace of God be with you," said the bishop.

"And with you, my lord," said Jerome.

"And so you are Jerome the hermit," said the bishop. "I have long wished to see you."

"And now you do see me, my lord," said Jerome bluntly, "a plain man who cannot understand why he has been summoned to Rome!"

"That I will explain," said the bishop. He seemed amused at his visitor's bruskness. "But first tell me about yourself."

"There is little to tell, my lord," said Jerome. "I am a priest and something of a scholar."

"Your humility does you credit, Father Jerome," said the bishop. "But there is much about you which we find of interest." He picked up a sheaf of papers from the desk and opened them.

"What are those papers, my lord?" Jerome asked.

"We always keep a record of the activities of the

more interesting members of the church," said the bishop. He read the page before him rapidly. "I see you were educated here in Rome; you studied law and philosophy. You also took a particular interest in the Pope's work in the catacombs, the caverns where the early Christians were buried."

Father Jerome looked long at the bishop before he said: "I understand why the Pope acted as he did, restoring the graves of the early Christian martyrs. It is to such great men as St. Peter and St. Paul, and a host of good men like them, that we owe everything." Jerome paused for a second and then looked again at the scarlet-robed bishop. "They were true Christians, brave men who lived simply, glad to suffer for Our Lord's sake. Today the leaders of the Church live like princes in great palaces in silken robes, my lord!"

A smile flickered across the face of the bishop. "They say that you are very outspoken, Father Jerome," he said. He glanced at the page in front of him. "I see you have traveled much. Then you went into the desert in the north of Palestine to live for six years as a hermit."

"That was because I renounced everything which kept me from God," said Jerome. "A man must live simply to understand the message of Our Lord. So I lived on wild fruits and herbs and drank nothing but a little brackish water. I suffered the heat of the day and the cold of the night gladly."

"You had books with you?"

"I studied ancient Hebrew, my lord, so that I could see where errors had been made in the Bible by careless copying. I read the writings of the great Origen, and translated some of his Hexapla from Greek into Latin."

The bishop watched Jerome, and nodded his head in agreement.

"We have heard," said the bishop, "that no one is your equal in knowledge of Hebrew and Greek. That is why I was commanded to summon you here."

"You were *commanded* to summon me?" said Jerome, looking sharply at the bishop.

"Yes, by the Holy Father himself."

"By the Pope?" said Jerome. He sprang up so quickly that the stool he had been sitting on fell over. "Then why did you not say so before?"

"Because, Father Jerome," said the bishop gently, "I wanted to find out what you were like. They say, for instance, that you are quarrelsome and have a quick temper."

"And you believe that tale?" said Jerome. His face began to go red and he clenched his hands. "Bad tempered? Me?" he asked. "What an absurd thing to say! Just because bad scholarship and careless work make me angry; just because I lose my patience with fools who criticize my books! Let me tell you," he shouted, "that if I could meet the man who told you that I was bad tempered I would soon make him change his tune." Jerome stood glaring at the bishop.

The door opened and a young monk looked in anxiously.

"Is anything amiss, my lord?" he said.

"No, nothing at all," said the bishop. "Father Jerome is just explaining to me that he is not quick-tempered."

The monk looked at Jerome and shut the door.

"I will tell you why His Holiness wanted you here," said the bishop calmly. "Here are three copies of part of the letter St. Paul wrote to Timothy of Ephesus, when he was here in Rome three hundred years ago. They are all very beautiful books, as you can see. Yet each is different in this passage at the top of the page. There is a dispute among the learned scholars who advise His Holiness as to which is correct. Which do you say is the correct version of St. Paul's letter?"

Jerome picked up the first book and looked at it. It was written on fine parchment, with beautiful lettering. But Jerome paid no attention to the beauty of the page. Instead, he read the first dozen lines and then threw the volume down.

"It is bad, very bad," he said. "Those were not the words of the blessed St. Paul! Some scribe has so altered them in copying that the sense is quite lost."

"Then is this one a true version?" asked the bishop, giving Jerome another book. This too was exquisitely written and decorated. Jerome glanced at it and threw it on to the desk.

"It is even worse than the other," he said. "A scribe has had the impudence to add words of his own."

"Then perhaps this is a true version," said the bishop, giving him the third book. "The workmanship is even more beautiful than the others, as you see."

"Pretty drawings at the side, my lord, and artistic lettering may look very fine, but it is the truth of the words that matters. And in this, my lord, there are as many errors as in the others. They are all false. These are not the words of St. Paul!"

The bishop picked up a small silver bell and rang it, and the young monk came into the room.

"Please ask the Secretary if His Holiness would see Father Jerome now," he said. The monk went out.

"What! Am I to see the Pope?" said Jerome.

"It is his wish. You can tell His Holiness what you think of these versions of St. Paul's epistle."

"Why did you not tell me this at once?" said Jerome. "You summon me here, you tell me I have a bad temper, you show me false texts of St. Paul, and then you tell me that the Pope himself wants to see me. I like plain dealing!"

"Come, calm yourself, Father Jerome!" said the bishop.

The door opened and the young monk said, "His Holiness will receive Father Jerome in the library, my lord."

"Come with me," said the bishop. He led Jerome

out of the room and down a corridor into a long room lined with books. At the far end an old man was standing before a tall reading desk. He turned as they approached. The bishop and Jerome stopped and bowed.

"This is Father Jerome, your Holiness," said the bishop.

Jerome went forward, dropped on his knees and kissed the ring on the Pope's hand.

"Bless you, my son," said the Pope, making a sign for Jerome to stand up. "You are very welcome. Have you seen the three texts of the Epistle of the blessed Saint Paul? We are in some confusion of mind about them."

"Yes, yes, I have seen them, Holy Father," said Jerome.

"And which do you say is the true version?"

Jerome, awed by the presence of the Pope, looked at the bishop.

"Father Jerome considers that all three of them are false, your Holiness," the bishop said.

The Pope looked surprised. "But they are all ancient versions," he said. "They are considered to be of great sanctity. How can they all be false?"

"Holy Father," said Jerome, "as in so much of the Scriptures, the true authentic word is lost beneath errors of copyists, and is marred by unworthy additions made by well-meaning men of little learning and less sense. They are worthless, quite worthless."

"My son," said the Pope, "I admire your candor, though I deplore what you say. Yet I fear it is the truth. In this library we have thousands of copies of the books of the Bible, and everywhere there is disagreement between them. Learned scholars quarrel over which is right. Where lies the truth?"

"The truth, Holy Father, lies in the earliest copies," said Jerome.

"And they have perished, or are worn out with handling and much reading. There is one way though," the Pope said, looking at Jerome, "and that is for some learned man to collect the oldest Latin versions he can find, compare them with the Hebrew for the Old Testament, with the most accurate Greek versions for the New, and then to write them all out again in Latin, the language the Western world understands."

"That would be too great a task for one man, Holy Father," said Jerome.

"There is only one man," said the Pope, "only one man who would let no word pass until he was sure it was the right one." The Pope looked at Jerome. The bishop looked at him as well. There was silence in the great library.

"Well, my son," said the Pope quietly, "will you do it?"

"It is so great a task, Holy Father," said Jerome.

"With God's blessing, and your own faith, my son, you could do it. Only think! The Holy Bible written anew in Latin; a true translation, to last for all time."

Jerome raised his head and looked at the Pope. "With God's help, Holy Father, and with your blessing, I will attempt it!" he said.

The Pope sighed, as though a great load were lifted from his heart.

"You will have God's help, my son, and my blessing, and indeed the blessing of all Christians throughout the world. And I know that you will accomplish this great task, to the glory of God, and through it you will yourself attain glory, most blessed Jerome."

As he spoke the Pope raised his hand in blessing, and Jerome and the bishop knelt. A shaft of sunlight, shining through a tall narrow window, fell on Jerome's head, like a halo of golden light.

Jerome began with the four Gospels, studying and rejecting countless Latin versions, and then wrote them out anew in Latin. Then he wrote out the rest of the New Testament, reading many versions, as Origen had done, examining every phrase and searching patiently to find which was true. Then he translated the Psalms.

When the Pope died, Jerome went to Bethlehem and continued his work in a large cave which was then believed to be next to the actual place where Jesus was born. He had a number of helpers, some of them women from the nearby convent. He wrote out all the Old Testament, translating it from ancient Hebrew into magnificent Latin.

The work took him more than twenty years, but at last it was done. After he died he was canonized and became Saint Jerome. Jerome's Latin Bible, which is called the Vulgate, was used by Christians everywhere for more than a thousand years, until it was translated into other languages. It is still used by many Roman Catholics today.

Note: In this story of the early Catholic Church, Paul is referred to as *Saint Paul* for he would have been so called by the characters in the story.

CHAPTER V

The Bible in English

We now go from Rome to England and step forward a thousand years in time. One Sunday afternoon in November, 1390, two men, Mr. Smith and Mr. Tandy, were walking briskly along a country lane near Leicester. Mr. Smith made wheels and Mr. Tandy kept an inn. Other groups of people were going the same way, which was rather strange because it was only a rough lane with no town or village in sight. At a point where a field path crossed the lane a tall young man in a scholar's gown joined Mr. Smith and Mr. Tandy.

"Well met, Master Norris," said Smith.

"Good day to you, Mr. Smith," said the young scholar.

"I am glad we have met you," said Mr. Smith, "for I have brought a friend, Richard Tandy. He has come to join us."

"Good day to you, sir," said Norris, looking shrewdly at the innkeeper. "You know, of course, that the business on which we meet this afternoon is likely to put you in peril?"

"I do indeed," said Tandy. "I have given my word to tell no one about it."

"I can vouch for my friend," said Smith.

"Good," said the scholar. "Tell me, Master Tandy, why have you come?"

Mr. Tandy thought for a minute. Then he said, "I

have noticed a sort of excitement in my neighbor Smith lately. I asked him the reason, so he has brought me to hear this new wonder with my own ears."

"You need not fear that my neighbor will betray us, Master Norris," said Smith. Then he added, "But I wondered if we should meet this afternoon as usual, now that the Archbishop of Canterbury himself has come to Leicester to prevent us."

"As for that," said Norris, "look, more people than ever before are going to the barn!"

Soon they arrived at an isolated barn hidden in a fold in the land. Bales of straw had been arranged to make seats. Smith and Tandy sat down and Norris went to the end of the barn where a man was arranging a great leather-bound book on a roughly made reading desk. A number of people were talking quietly together in groups.

"What happens?" Tandy asked.

"When everyone has come," said Smith, "Master Norris will read a passage from the Bible in English. He is a clever scholar and can read as easily as you or I can talk. Then we shall all sing a psalm. It will be written out in English on sheets of paper which are passed round to those who can read. One of the men with Master Norris leads the singing. Then we shall all pray together."

"In English?"

"Assuredly. It is all in our own tongue, that is what

is so wonderful. Nothing is in Latin. You will understand every word."

"Look," said Mr. Tandy, "there is Giles the miller and his wife, and over there Francis the pastrycook."

"All manner of men and women come," said Mr. Smith, "rich and poor, scholars and unlettered folk. Hush, they are closing the doors."

Silence fell in the barn, and everyone looked expectantly at Norris. He stood at the reading desk and prayed silently. Then he opened his eyes.

"Brethren," he said, "may God bless our meeting. The great men of the Church say we should not read the Bible in the English tongue. They say our church services must only be in Latin. But we do not understand Latin."

"In coming here all are breaking the law of the Archbishop and the Princes of our church, because they have expressly forbidden us to meet like this. So if any of you feels that it is wrong to read God's Word in English, let him now go from hence."

People looked round uneasily, but no one moved.

"For my part, I am convinced that we do no wrong," went on Norris. "The Old Testament was first written in Hebrew for the Hebrew people. The Gospels and the Letters were written in Greek, for that was the language the early Christians spoke. Later, the Bible and the Mass were written in Latin, for people spoke Latin. We are English. I will now read in English from the fifth chapter of the Gospel According to St. Matthew. It is a special message for humble folk who worship God in peril."

There was a rustle of straw as the people settled to listen. Norris began to read in the simple and homely English of the translation made by John Wycliffe.

" 'And Jesus, seeing the people, went up into an hill, and when he was set his disciples came to him. And he opened his mouth and taught them and said, Blessed are men poor in spirit for the Kingdom of Heaven is theirs. Blessed are mild men, for they shall weld (have power over) the earth. Blessed are they that mourn, for they shall be comforted. Blessed are they that hunger and thirst for righteousness for they shall be fulfilled. Blessed are the merciful men, for they shall get mercy. Blessed are they that are of clean heart, for they shall see God. Blessed are peaceable men, for they shall be called God's children.' "

Norris raised his voice and glanced up at the people sitting in front of him.

" 'Blessed are they that suffer persecution for righteousness, for the Kingdom of Heaven is theirs. You shall be blessed when men shall curse you and shall pursue you and shall say all evil against you, lying, for me. Joy ye and be glad, for your meed (reward) is plentous in heaven, for so they have pursued also prophets that were before you.' "

The strong voice of the reader filled the barn, and

51

everyone sat silent, listening eagerly, to the wonderful words for the first time in his own language.

While Norris was reading the Bible in English, thirty horsemen were trotting along a country lane. The pale November sunlight shone on their polished breastplates and helmets. They rode two by two in perfect order, for they were well-trained soldiers. An officer rode at the head of the column on a fine white horse. His breastplate was inlaid with gilt, a long red plume nodded from his helm, and his coat of arms was painted on his shield. His vizor was up to show a weather-beaten face and a thick black moustache. At his side rode a priest, a lean young man.

"How much farther to this barn?" asked the officer.

"Oh, we shall not be there for a quarter of an hour yet, Sir William," said the priest.

The knight turned in his saddle to see that his men were riding in proper formation. Two who had been talking stopped at once.

"How did you find out about this forbidden meeting?" Sir William asked.

"Oh, that was easy," said the priest. "One of my spies overheard a conversation in Leicester Market. He told me of this secret meeting and I told the Archbishop. He sent for you to arrest them."

"I see," said the knight. "What sort of people are they?"

"Oh, ordinary people, Sir William. His Grace will

put them in prison for a few days, then give them the opportunity to win his pardon by doing penance. But the fate of the leaders will be harder, much harder," the priest added grimly.

"It doesn't seem very wicked, just to listen to someone reading the Bible in English," said the knight.

"There, Sir William, you speak without knowledge. It is most dangerous; the Archbishop is determined to stop it. The priests can understand Latin, and that is sufficient. The common people can see the pictures painted on the church walls and have the Bible explained to them by the priests, who have the knowledge to understand such sacred matters."

"That's true," said Sir William, "Latin is the proper language for church, even if you don't understand it. The Bible wouldn't seem right in English."

"It certainly does not sound right!" said the priest. "The sacred book is not for ignorant people to read. John Wycliffe started all this trouble."

"Ah, he was a most learned man, they say," said Sir William. He turned in his saddle and looked down the column. "Close up in the rear there," he roared, "don't straggle!"

"John Wycliffe was assuredly most learned," said the priest. "A very clever priest, and Master of Balliol College, Oxford. But he had the most outrageous ideas. Unfortunately many people listened to him, even great princes and nobles. Wycliffe dared to say that it was wrong for Englishmen to pay taxes to the Pope in Rome! He sent out his 'poor priests,' to travel like beggars round the land, teaching his dangerous doctrine. But it was a bad day for us when he translated the Bible from Latin into the common English tongue."

"But what a tremendous work, to translate the whole Bible," said Sir William.

"He had friends who helped him. It has been copied hundreds of times. The common people clamor to read it. It does great harm. It upsets the people and encourages them to criticize the Church and us, the priests. It is worse here in Leicestershire than anywhere else, for Wycliffe was the Rector of Lutterworth, nearby. The Archbishop of Canterbury has come to Leicester especially to stamp out this reading of the Bible in English once and for all. And there, Sir William," he said, pointing, "is the barn."

Sir William held up his arm and the column halted. He rode forward alone to examine the countryside, trotted back and gave his orders crisply. The horsemen cantered off to right and to left until they made a ring around the barn. At a signal from Sir William they walked their horses inward, dismounted, tethered their horses to the trees and formed up.

From the barn came the sound of singing.

"Listen to them," said the priest scornfully, "they are chanting a psalm in English! How dreadful it sounds after the beauty of Latin. Sir William, to your duty! See that no one escapes."

Sir William gave his final orders. Half a dozen soldiers were posted to catch anyone who tried to escape. Two went to the barn doors, others formed up behind their officer. Sir William glanced at the priest, who gave a curt nod. The two soldiers flung open the barn doors and Sir William and the priest strode in.

The voices ceased and the people turned toward the opened doors. When they saw Sir William and the soldiers they looked round them in dismay. Then Norris started to sing again, loud and bold, and gradually the people joined in.

The priest strode forward. "Cease this noise," he shouted. "In the name of the Archbishop of Canterbury, cease, I say!"

The chanting died down for a moment and then swelled up again. "Our God, thou our refuge and strength, helper in tribulations that have come upon us greatly. Therefore we shall not dread, while the earth shall be disturbed, and the hills shall be borne over into the heart of the sea."

It did not last long. The soldiers seized the people and dragged them outside. A few tried to resist but that only brought them rougher treatment. Soon Norris was alone, looking upward and chanting the psalm boldly. Two soldiers seized his arms and shook him. The priest walked up to him.

"What is your name?" he asked.

"Richard Norris."

"So you are Richard Norris," said the priest. "I have heard of you. You were once a scholar of Oxford, and now you are a follower of Wycliffe, one of those rascals we call Lollards!"

"I was indeed once a scholar of Oxford," said Norris, "and now I am proud to be called a Lollard and proud to follow the teaching of the great John Wycliffe!"

"Know you not," said the priest, "that the Archbishop has forbidden reading the Bible in English?"

"Assuredly I know it."

"Then how dare you defy the authority of his Grace?"

"Because the Bible, the Word of God, is mightier than the Archbishop, Sir Priest," said Norris. "Did not St. Paul write, 'for whatever things are written those are written to our teaching, that by patience and comfort of Scriptures we have hope'?"

The priest looked angrily at Norris and then said to the soldiers: "Take him outside with the others." He picked up the great leather-bound Bible. "This I shall take for the Archbishop, and he will have it burned on a bonfire. The Bible in English, forsooth!"

"You may burn the book," said Norris as the soldiers took him away, "but you will not stop people from reading God's word in their own language!"

As they took Norris outside he smiled cheerfully at

the people standing in twilight amid the soldiers.

"Be of good cheer, my friends," he said. "Remember what I read to you: 'Blessed are they that suffer persecution for righteousness, for the Kingdom of Heaven is theirs. You shall be blessed when men shall curse you and shall pursue you.' So brethren, we can be of good cheer!"

"Silence, you impious Lollard," shouted the priest.

The soldiers mounted their horses. The prisoners, their hands tied behind them, walked between the horsemen through the dusk of that November evening. Heartened by the words of Norris they held their heads high.

"What will happen to them?" Sir William asked the priest as they rode behind the column.

"They will spend tonight in prison," said the priest. "Tomorrow they will be taken before the Archbishop. They will be given a hard penance to perform and warned against ever reading or listening to the Bible in English. But as for Master Norris, his lot will be harder! I expect his Grace will sentence him to serve all his days in the monastery, in perpetual silence. And this book —why, it will be burned."

That is how, in the fourteenth century, the Church tried to stop people reading the Bible in English.

Note: The scripture Master Norris read to the people (Matt. 5:1-12) and quoted as he was being taken prisoner

(Rom. 15:4), as well as the psalm the people chanted (Ps. 46), were from Wycliffe's Bible, the first complete Bible to be written in English. The spelling given here has been modernized. Most copies of Wycliff's Bible were destroyed. Some were kept hidden in chests or cupboards to be examined or read only when doors were locked. People learned whole passages or even whole chapters by heart and recited them to their friends.

John Foxe, the author of the *Book of Martyrs*, writing about Wycliffe's Bible a century and a half later, in the reign of Queen Elizabeth I, wrote: "The fervent zeal of those Christian days seemed much superior to these our days and times; as manifestly may appear by their sitting up all night in reading and hearing; also by their expenses in buying books in English. Some gave five marks, some more, some less, for a book: some gave a load of hay for a few chapters of St. James or St. Paul in English."

By "books in English" Foxe meant Wycliffe's Bible. The five marks which some people paid for a copy would be approximately $112 in United States currency.

"Lollards," the name given to followers of Wycliffe, was probably applied to the English group because in action and belief they resembled certain European groups, also called Lollards, who protested the complete authority of the pope and the worldliness of the church. In the fourteenth century throughout Europe there was unrest and dissension against the church.

CHAPTER VI

Smugglers' Bible

One day in the year 1523 some gentlemen sat in a manor house in Gloucestershire, chatting after supper. The house belonged to Sir John Walsh, and among his guests were a bishop and a London merchant. The merchant and the bishop were arguing about the Church in England, and the others joined in, some on the merchant's side and some on the bishop's.

"I am surprised," said Sir John Walsh after a while, "that Master Tyndale sits silent at the lower end of the table there. These are matters on which I know he holds strong views."

"Indeed," said the bishop, "and who is Master Tyndale?"

They all looked toward the man who sat silent, crumbling bread into pellets.

"William Tyndale is the tutor to my children," said Sir John, "and an excellent tutor, too. He is notably learned in Greek and Latin."

"I hope you do not hold the same outrageous views as our friend the merchant here," said the bishop to Tyndale.

"I do, my lord," said Tyndale. "I fear that much that the priests teach the people is not in accordance with the teaching of Our Lord Jesus Christ. Men should be able to read God's Word for themselves. The Bible should be written in English."

"Oh, that old tale!" said the bishop with a smile. "That would never do! The Bible is in Latin and must remain so. Why, John Wycliffe wrote the Bible in English a hundred and fifty years ago, and what happened to it?"

"Every copy of Wycliffe's Bible which the Church could lay hands on was destroyed, my lord," said Tyndale, "and men and women were punished for reading it. But there is a great difference between those days and these. The printing press has been invented. If the Bible were translated into English now, it could be printed. Thousands of copies could be made, each exactly the same. Then men could read God's word for themselves, and not rely only on what they are told by the priests."

The bishop was no longer smiling; an angry flush had spread over his cheeks. "Your ideas are absurd, Master Tyndale, and highly dangerous," he said sharply. "The Church, under the Pope in Rome, is supreme. There is no need for people to read the Bible themselves."

"My lord bishop," said Tyndale, standing up, "I agree that the Pope is supreme in the Church. But it is the Word of God, as written in the Holy Bible, which comes first. It is only right that all men should read it for themselves. And, my lord," he said, standing straight and looking directly at the bishop, "if God spare my life, I will translate the Bible into English, so that the boy that drives the plow shall know more

61

of the Scriptures than you do!" He bowed to Sir John and the company and strode out of the great hall.

A quarter of an hour later the merchant found Tyndale leaning against a mulberry tree in the garden.

"So this is where you are, young man," said the merchant. "You startled the bishop well enough!"

"I thought it best to leave the company, sir," said Tyndale. "I was, I fear, somewhat outspoken."

"I would that more would be as bold! Now, tell me frankly, do you really believe that it would be right to print the Bible in English?"

"I am sure of it, sir," said Tyndale.

"And have you sufficient knowledge to do such a great work?"

"I could do my utmost, sir. Erasmus of Rotterdam has compiled a new version of the New Testament in Greek from old texts. He has had it printed, so I could use a copy. I would compare that Greek version with the Latin, and write it in English, and have it printed. Then I would translate the Old Testament. To such a work I would gladly devote my whole life, aye and die for it if need be!"

The merchant looked at Tyndale for a moment. Then he put a hand on his shoulder. "Master Tyndale," he said, "you must do this work! Translate the Bible into English, and have it printed!"

"But how can it be done?" said Tyndale. "It would be necessary to rent a house, buy a printing press, pay printers, buy paper and boards for the covers—it could cost a great deal of money."

"Do not worry about money. I know many wealthy merchants like myself who would gladly find the money for so worthy a work."

"I would not be allowed to do it, sir," said Tyndale sadly. "The bishops would have me arrested. They would destroy the printing press, and burn the books."

"Then you must go abroad," said the merchant. "Go to Germany; you will be safe there. I will arrange it. Translate the Bible there and print it, and we will devise means to get the books into England. Come, Master Tyndale, what say you?"

Tyndale took his hand. "Sir," he said, "I will do it, God helping me."

"Splendid! Come, let us walk in the orchard and talk of ways and means."

Tyndale began his work in London, but it soon became apparent that it would be impossible to complete the task, or even make any real progress, where the project was so bitterly opposed by both church and state. As his merchant-benefactor had first suggested, he went to Germany.

Three years later a sturdy man, wearing a dark blue cloak, walked down a street of the city of Cologne in Germany. Every now and then he looked at a piece of paper in his hand, and then at the houses. Eventually he stopped in front of a house, looked at the piece of paper again, and then knocked on the door. It was opened by a young man who was wiping his inky fingers on a cloth.

"Good day to you," said the man in the dark blue cloak. "I was told to bring this letter to this house."

"Ah, yes. Come in, sir," said the young man.

"The saints be praised that you talk English," said the visitor as he went in.

"But of course, sir, we are all English here. May I see your letter, please?"

He looked at the paper, examined the signature, and handed it back. "We have to be very careful, sir," he explained, "as you probably know. Come."

The room was full of books; they were stacked on the floor and on the long table. Pages were laid out on the table in piles, and there was a large pot of glue and strips of canvas, ready for binding the pages into books.

"So you are Captain Nicholas Ball," said the young man.

"Master of the Neptune," said the sea captain.

"Master Tyndale will be here presently," said the young man. "He is watching them set up another page on the printing press."

"This is all a mystery to me," said Captain Ball. "I was given this address in Cologne and made to promise to tell no one of my errand. They also warned me to be sure that I was not followed. I understand you have some cargo for my ship, to be taken to England."

64

"It is very special merchandise," said the young man, "to be hidden in bales of cloth and sacks of grain."

"I was told that this is a hazardous business," said Captain Ball, "and I confess that I have been very uneasy. I am a law-abiding sea captain, young man, and I take care not to fall foul of the law. This sounds like some treasonable business, and I don't like it. It is only because I respect the owner of my ship that I have come. I'll do nothing treasonable. What is this cargo?"

"There is your cargo, Captain," said the young man, pointing to the stacks of books on the floor.

"Books!" said the captain, astonished. "But why should there be such secrecy about a cargo of books?" "Are they treasonable? Against the King's Majesty?"

"Take one, Captain, and see for yourself."

Captain Ball picked up the top book of a pile. "It is handsomely bound," he said. He opened the book at random and read aloud the passage at the top of the page: " 'Though I speak with the tongues of men and angels,' " he read, " 'and yet had no love I were even as sounding brass and as a tinkling cymbal; and though I could prophesy and understand all secrets—and all knowledge, yea if I had all faith—so that I could move mountains out of their places and yet had no love, I were nothing.' "

The captain looked up. "This is magnificent, magnificent! I have never read the like!"

"It is part of the First Letter of St. Paul to the Corinthians. It is the beginning of the thirteenth chapter," said the young man. (The passage is from Tyndale's translation of I Corinthians, chapter 13, verses 1 and 2, with modernized spelling.)

"You mean, it is from the Bible?"

"That book, captain, is the New Testament of the Holy Bible."

"But it is printed in English!"

"Master Tyndale has translated it and we print it here on the press in the back room. I am binding the copies on the table."

The captain looked at the book in his hands and then round the room. "The New Testament, in English! But why do you print here in Germany?"

"Because it would not be permitted in England. The Church authorities would break up the press and destroy the books. Even here we have to be careful; their spies are hunting for us. So the New Testaments have to be smuggled into England."

"So that is why there is such secrecy!" said the captain. "Could I have a copy to read in my cabin?"

"I am sure that can be arranged. But here comes Master Tyndale."

"I see we have a visitor," said William Tyndale when he came in.

"Nicholas Ball, Master of the Neptune, at your service," said the captain, bowing.

"You are most welcome, Captain," said Tyndale.

"Has my friend explained what your cargo is to be?"

"He has," said the captain, "and I have glanced at this copy. It is magnificent, sir, magnificent!"

"What a marvel this printing press is, Captain," said Tyndale. "That page before you would take a scholar a whole day to write out. To write out the whole New Testament once would take a man—how long? Two years? Three years? Yet in a few months we have printed three thousand copies, all exactly alike."

"It is a marvel indeed," said the captain. "Now that you have printed the New Testament, will you do the Old Testament too?"

"God willing, yes. That is my intention. But we are beset with difficulties. One of them is getting the books to England. That is why I am so glad to see you."

"I will do exactly as you instruct me," the captain said.

"The books will be taken by a wagon to the dock where your ship lies. My men will stow them deep inside sacks of grain and bales of cloth, marking the sacks and bales with this secret sign." Tyndale made a mark on a piece of paper for the captain to see. "You must stow those sacks and bales among the rest of the cargo in your ship's hold, so that they are well hidden. When you get to England an official may come on board, with a warrant from the Bishop of London to search your ship. There may be spies of the Bishop on the dock, so you must be very careful."

"I will be careful, Master Tyndale, have no fear."

"When your cargo is unloaded in England our men will open the marked bales and take the books to London or to Oxford. They will be hidden in bookshops, to be sold to those who will keep the secret."

"There must be many engaged in this enterprise," said the captain.

"There are a great number of us, glad to risk imprisonment, and death if need be, to get these books to England."

"I am honored to be one of such a company, Master Tyndale," said the captain.

"You run a grave risk, Captain," said Tyndale.

"Have no fear for me, Master Tyndale," said the captain. "Whatever risk there is I take it gladly for this good work. And if there is risk for me, who only carry the books to England, what risk do you run!"

"We do not think of that," said Tyndale. "The work is all that matters. God be with you, Captain, and a fair wind for England!"

"God be with you, Master Tyndale," said the captain, "and God bless you and prosper your great enterprise. I am proud to have a hand in it."

Many ships sailed from Germany to England with copies of Tyndale's New Testament. Sometimes the bishop's spies found them, but more often they were safely delivered to bookshops in London or Oxford, hidden from prying eyes and sold to discreet people.

In Germany the bishop's spies hunted for Tyndale and his printing press. Several times he was warned by a friend only just in time to escape. He moved from city to city, working without rest at translating the Bible into English and printing the books.

The bishops in England were very angry. Not only was Tyndale successfully defying their authority in publishing the New Testament in English, but he had put notes in the margin saying sharp things about the Church of Rome, about priests and even about the Pope himself. Tyndale's New Testament was publicly declared to be a wicked book and people were forbidden to own or read it. To get rid of the hated copies of the New Testament some of the bishops used their own money to buy every copy they could find, and they burned them all with great pomp and ceremony on a huge bonfire at St. Paul's Cathedral.

They thought that the bonfire would put an end to the English New Testaments, but the result was exactly the opposite. The money paid by the bishops was sent to Tyndale in Germany and it arrived just when he needed it most. With the money he was able to print a new and larger edition of the New Testament. As before, the books were smuggled into England, and bought and read eagerly by people all over the country.

Tyndale also began work on the Old Testament, and by 1530 he had translated the first five books, from Genesis to Deuteronomy. He printed and bound them, and they, too, were smuggled into England, in spite of the strenuous efforts of the bishops to stop them.

The extraordinary thing was that not only did Tyndale have the knowledge to translate the Bible into English, and the skill and energy to print his books, but he wrote his translations in wonderful English. His New Testament had the purity and loveliness of language of the Greek, and his Old Testament the majesty and dignity of the ancient Hebrew. Englishmen were delighted to be able to read the Bible in their own language, but they were also awed and inspired by the grandeur of the English in which it was written.

At last, in 1535, Tyndale was caught. A spy tracked him down and he was kidnapped and thrown into prison in a fortress at Villevorde in Belgium. But he did not despair. In his bitterly cold and damp dungeon, with barely enough food to keep him alive, he went on with his work. In the sixteen months he spent in the dungeon he finished translating nine more books of the Old Testament, to the end of the Second Book of Chronicles. He could not get them printed, of course, but they were smuggled out and printed later.

The end of the great man's life came on Friday, October 6th, 1536. On that morning the Governor of the prison went to Tyndale's dungeon, accompanied by several jailers. Tyndale knew why they had come.

"Good morrow, my friends," he said. "You have come for me?"

"We have," said the Governor of the prison. "Pray make yourself ready to die."

Tyndale looked at the Governor for a moment and then said, simply, "I am ready."

"Master Tyndale," said the Governor, "it is the custom to grant a condemned man a last wish."

"My last wish?" said Tyndale. "Why, it is a prayer; that the people of England may be allowed to read the Bible in English. It is simply this—"Lord, open the King of England's eyes!'"

Those were Tyndale's last words. He was strangled, and then burned at the stake. They said he was a heretic, and enemy of the Church. Two years later his last prayer was answered. King Henry VIII issued a Royal decree. It was that "one book of the whole Bible in the largest volume in English" was to be set up in every church in the realm.

It is said that Tyndale's writings helped to shape the thinking of the Puritans in England.

> Note: At the time of Tyndale's residence on the Continent all of Western Europe was watching with growing interest the life and writings of Martin Luther, one of the leaders of the religious revolution, the Reformation, which was to bring about worldwide changes resulting in two main bodies of Christian thought and teaching: Protestant and Catholic. It is thought that before Tyndale settled in Cologne, he had visited Luther in Wittenberg.

CHAPTER VII

"A Treasury of Most Costly Jewels"

During the last years of Tyndale's life events of the greatest importance were happening in England. The majority of Englishmen had for a long time resented the domination of the Pope in far-off Italy. This resentment was brought to a head in 1534 when King Henry VIII quarreled with the Pope. The authority of Rome was abolished in England and the King became "Head of the Church." The monasteries, which had been an important part of the life of the country for centuries, were destroyed. Gradually England became free from the authority of Rome and the control of the Pope.

For our story, the most important change was the adoption of the Bible in English. No longer did people have to read the Bible secretly, for an English Bible was put in every church in the land.

A friend of Tyndale's, Miles Coverdale, printed large numbers of Tyndale's Bible, and he himself translated those books of the Old Testament that Tyndale had not had time to finish. Six different translations were made and printed in the thirty years after Tyndale's death. It was said that "England became the land of one book, and that book the Bible." Men and women learned to read so that they could read the Bible, and they governed their lives by its teaching.

When King James I came to the throne in 1603 one

of the first things he did was to hold a conference on religion at Hampton Court. Among those participating in the conference were representatives of the group of people known as Puritans. Although in America the word "Puritan" would come to designate rather generally the people who first settled its New England shores, "Puritan" in England was a label for Englishmen who, about 1560, were seeking purification of the established church of England. The Puritans were urging a strict adherence to the Bible itself, as the final authority, rather than to church tradition or to rules made by priests or other church leaders.

After the conference at Hampton Court, King James discussed the matter with the Bishop of London.

"What do you think of the conference, my Lord Bishop?" the King asked.

"A great deal of good sense was talked, Your Majesty," replied the Bishop, "and much that was not so good."

"That is always the way with conferences," said the King. "But one thing emerged which is good, the need for a new translation of the Bible into English."

"But, sire," said the Bishop, "there are half a dozen English Bibles. Why should we have yet another?"

"For that very reason. There should be but one Bible, the most perfect and the nearest to the ancient Scriptures that we can obtain. Then shall the whole church be bound to one Bible and no other. It must contain the best of all the others, with the errors corrected."

"But Your Majesty," said the Bishop, "who has the learning to perform so great a task? The Bible of William Tyndale, and those that have come after it, are the careful work of profound scholars. What man has such knowledge that he can improve on them?"

"No single man could do it, my Lord Bishop," said the King, "but nevertheless it can be done—by many scholars working together."

"But sire, you know how it is with learned men, they delight to dispute and argue over trifles. The work would never be finished."

"It will be finished," said the King, picking up a sheet of paper. "I have worked out the method. A number of scholars will be divided into six groups. Two groups will work at Oxford, two at Cambridge, and two here in Westminster. Each group will be given a part of the Bible to work on."

"Your Majesty has worked out the whole scheme!" said the Bishop, partly to flatter the King, but partly in genuine admiration.

"Oh, there is more yet," the King said. "When one group has translated a book of the Bible, a copy will be sent to each of the other groups. They will examine it, and return it with any improvements they can suggest. Finally, when all is done, six of the best scholars, one from each group, will meet here in London and examine again the whole work. The approved version will then be examined in turn by the bishops, by the Privy Council, and lastly by me. Then we shall have a Bible as nearly true to the ancient texts as scholarship and care can make it. Well, my Lord Bishop, what say you?"

"It is a magnificent scheme, Your Majesty, and with God's blessing we shall give the people of this realm the Scriptures in English, as true as may be."

"Now, Bishop," said the King, "prepare a list of the best Hebrew and Greek scholars in the land. We must appoint a master for each group."

The work was started in 1607, and it was done exactly as King James had planned. Fifty-four learned men worked in six teams. Two teams met in Cambridge, two in Oxford, and two in London. They compared all the earlier versions of the English Bible and examined them sentence by sentence, word by word. They tried always to find the true meaning of the Hebrew or Greek and to translate it into the right English word or phrase. The Greek scholars studied and corrected any mistakes of translation in the New Testament, the Hebrew scholars did the same for the Old Testament.

The different groups then examined each other's work and tested it carefully, making any further corrections. They worked hard for three years, and wrote out the whole Bible so that the English version was as true to the original as they could make it. The new Bible was printed in 1611 and was called the Authorized Version, because it was authorized by the King. In America

it is known as the King James Version of the Bible.

Many passages of the earlier English versions were kept because they could not be improved. The greatness of the work of William Tyndale is shown by the fact that nearly four-fifths of the King James Version is in the words and phrases Tyndale wrote.

The Bible of King James has been in use ever since and it is read by millions of English-speaking people all over the world. It did much to form our character, and its language became part of our everyday speech.

The King James Version was translated when the English language was at its best, the language of Shakespeare. That is why the translators of King James wrote their English Bible in the splendid language which has inspired men, women, and children for three hundred years and more. In the introduction to the first edition in 1611 the Bible was described as "a treasury of most costly jewels."

When you hear the Bible read to you, or when you read it yourself, listen to the splendor of the language. And remember the long story behind your Bible. Remember the men who wrote the books so long ago, and the early Christian martyrs. Remember Origen and Jerome and Wycliffe, and the men who wrote and read the Bible in peril of prison. Remember William Tyndale, who was killed because he translated and printed the Bible in English, and remember those careful scholars of King James. Treasure your Bible.

PART II

Reference Section

How to Find Out More About the Bible

The stories told in the first part of this book are made up, but they are all based on fact or on ancient tradition. This second part gives some of the facts about the Bible which will help you to understand how the Bible is put together and how it has come down to us through two thousand years.

CHAPTER I

What Is the Bible?

The word "Bible" means a collection of books, or to be exact, a collection of *the* books. That is just what the Bible is, a library of sixty-six books bound in one volume. They were written long ago at different times, but they all have one theme in common, the story of the coming of Christ. They are like different beads on one string.

The books of the Bible are an historical record of the most important events in all human history, because they tell us how God revealed His purpose to man. The Old Testament books are about God and the Children of Israel, the people chosen by God. From the Old Testament we learn God's law, and the history of the Jews, the people among whom Christ was born. We also read of the coming of the Messiah, the Savior. The books of the New Testament tell the story of the life and teaching of Jesus Christ, whom Christians recognize as the Messiah. They also tell the story of the the early Christian Church, and the lives and adventures of the Apostles.

God's Covenant

The two parts of the Bible were once called the Old Covenant and the New Covenant. Covenant means agreement, and the Bible is about the covenant between God and man, the promise by God to care for us.

In return for that loving care man is to remain faithful and dedicated to God's plan and purposes. The change to the word "Testament" reminds us that God gives freely out of his goodness, as when someone leaves riches to another in his will and testament; and reminds us that God urges and expects us to live up to the terms of the covenant so that we may enjoy its bounty completely. If we remember that testament also means covenant, an agreement, we can understand better the message of the Bible.

The Old Testament

The books of the Old Testament tell how God promised to care for the Children of Israel. You can read that promise in Leviticus, chapter 26, verse 12. God says to Moses: "I will walk among you, and will be your God, and you shall be my people."

God's promise was shown when he inspired Moses to lead the people of Israel out of slavery in Egypt toward Canaan, the Promised Land. The great story of the rescue of the Jews from bondage was written down, and the Law which Moses gave them. Then the writers of the early books looked back to earlier times and saw another proof of God's care for their people in the life of Abraham, the father of their race. Then they looked farther back in history and wrote the story of Noah's preservation from the flood as a still earlier example of God's care. After that was written the story of the creation, in which it is shown that the God who watched over Israel was not one God among many, but the only God, who created the whole universe.

All the books in the Old Testament deal in one way or another with the influence of God over the Hebrews, first under their Judges or rulers, and then under their Kings.

Some books of the Old Testament contain poems and hymns in praise of God, others the writings of the prophets. These prophetic books were written by inspired men who could understand the meaning of the history of their times, and could see how God was at work carrying out His purpose. The prophets tried to keep the people true to God. In the prophetic books the writers often look forward to the coming of a Messiah, the "anointed Prince," sent from God, to lead them back to goodness.

The New Testament

The New Testament is the story of this Messiah, the Son of God, born into a simple Jewish family and taught from the Old Testament books. The Gospels are the record of the life and teaching of Jesus, His death and resurrection, and ascension into heaven. The other books in the New Testament tell of the development of the Christian Church. In the New Testament Jesus makes a new covenant, or promise; this time it is not only to the Jews but to all mankind.

The Jews had expected the Messiah to be a great prince, a splendid national leader who would free them from their Roman overlords. They could not recognize the son of the humble carpenter as the long-awaited Messiah. When Jesus declared that He was the Son of God, the priests of the Jews were shocked. His teaching angered them, especially when He said that God loved all men and was not only the God of the Jews. When the priests saw how the common people crowded to listen to Jesus, and believed in Him, they decided to kill Him.

The Bible is important because it is the history of great events written by people inspired to understand their meaning. The two principal events are God's promise to the Jews, the Old Covenant; and Christ's promise to all mankind, the New Covenant. All the books in the Bible refer in one way or another to these two great events. That is why the Bible is the most important book in human history. It is the chief guide to our Christian faith.

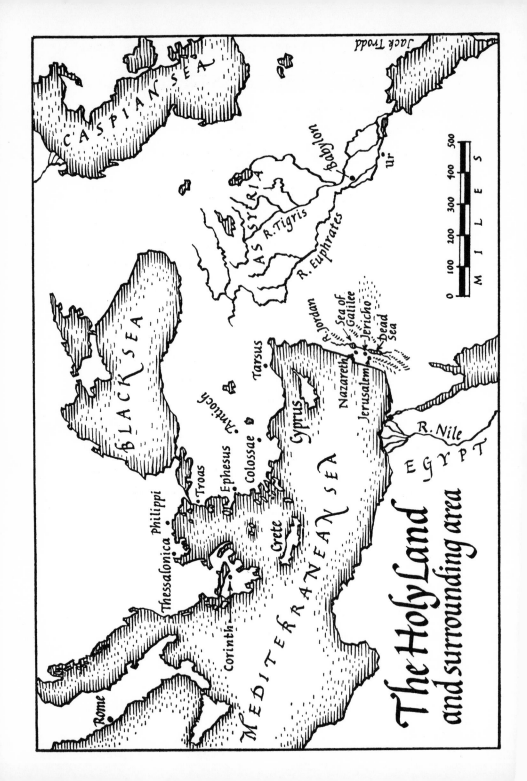

The Holy Land and surrounding area

Jack Trodd

CHAPTER II

The Land of the Bible

When the People of Israel were led into Canaan, where they were to make their home, Joshua took them into a small strip of country not much larger than the state of New Jersey. It is only about two hundreds fifty miles long and varies from forty to twenty-five miles in width. This is the center of Old Testament history, and it was here that Jesus lived.

Canaan, or Palestine as it was later called, lies at the eastern end of the Mediterranean, between the sea and desert of Arabia. It is divided into several strips of different kinds of country. First is the coastal plain, then the central plateau, and beyond that a long valley. This is the valley of the River Jordan which flows through the Sea of Galilee down to the Dead Sea, which is more than one thousand feet *below* sea level. East of the valley of the Jordan the land rises to a bleak wilderness of mountains, and beyond that lies the vast desert.

South of Palestine is Egypt, in Old Testament times a great and rich nation on the fertile banks of the Nile. To the north were the nations of Asia Minor, and to the northeast Mesopotamia, where, between the rivers Tigris and Euphrates, the two great kingdoms of Assyria and Babylon flourished.

Palestine was not in a comfortable position, a small nation lying between powerful ones, especially as it was the only route between Egypt and the north and east. That is why we read in the Old Testament of so many wars in which the Israelites, the residents of Palestine, had to fight invaders.

Palestine was an important part of the Roman Empire in New Testament times. Rome had to hold this vital link between its provinces in North Africa and Egypt, and the busy nations of Asia Minor. All the lands around the Mediterranean were part of the Roman Empire, which stretched westward to what is now Spain and France and beyond them to Britain.

The land of the Bible has always been a center of conflict. It is from that small and troubled land that we have the great literature of the Old Testament. It was there also that Jesus lived and died. And it was from Palestine that the Apostles set out on their journeys to spread the gospel.

CHAPTER III

When the Bible Was Written

No one knows with any certainty when the books of the Old Testament were written. Ancient religious writings have been discovered which might go back three thousand years before Christ. In ancient days the stories were often passed down orally, told again and again through the generations. When an ancient manuscript is discovered, no one knows how many copies of it had been made before that particular one.

Nevertheless scholars have devoted years of careful research to find out when Old Testament books were written, and the dates we have are as correct as scholarship can make them. If we will remember that the letters B.C. are used with the years *before* Christ and A.D. with the years beginning with his birth, the dates shown in the following paragraphs have greater meaning.

The Song of Deborah (in Judges, chapter 5) and parts of the Law of Moses were probably written before 1000 B.C.

Parts of the books from Genesis through Second Samuel were probably written about 950 B.C., and then were added to from time to time. Amos was the first of the prophets whose preaching was written down. He lived about 750 B.C. The Psalms and Proverbs probably were being collected over many centuries. The last of the Old Testament books is believed to have been written in the second century before the birth of Christ.

Our knowledge is more certain when we come to *translations* of the Old Testament and the writing of the New Testament:

250 B.C. to 150 B.C.	The writing of the Septuagint, the translation of the Old Testament into Greek.
A.D. 50 to A.D. 120	The books of the New Testament were written. First the letters of Paul and the Gospels of Mark, Matthew, and Luke, probably in that order and perhaps between A.D. 50 and A.D. 85. Among the last to be written were the Gospel of John and the Letters of John.
A.D. 150 to A.D. 200	Three important translations of the Old Testament were made, from Hebrew into Greek, by Aquila, Theodotion, and Symmachus.
A.D. 250	The Greek versions of the Old Testament were revised by Origen in his Hexapla or six-column version.

During the second and third centuries, first the New Testament and then the Old were translated from Greek into Latin. As Christianity spread a great number of copies of the Latin Bible were in use.

A.D. 404

St. Jerome finished his work on the Bible in Latin, the Vulgate.

CHAPTER IV

How the Bible Has Come Down to Us

The books of the Bible were first written between two and three thousand years ago! It is interesting to see how they have come down to us through all these years. The main reason for their survival is that they have been treasured as sacred books. But when were they written, and how have they been preserved over the centuries?

The Old Testament Books

The books of the Old Testament may have first been scratched on bits of pottery or clay or wood. Later they were written on prepared skin called parchment or on papyrus, a kind of paper made from the fiber of a plant. They were the Jewish Scriptures, and they were written in Hebrew.

The skin or papyrus books were written on long narrow strips. They varied from ten to twenty inches in height and they were very long, often as long as thirty feet.

The books were kept in the Jewish churches, the synagogues, and read by trained readers. When they wore out, new copies were made and the old books were stored away and eventually buried in jars in the ground or in caves, for the Jews would not destroy sacred books. Fragments of these ancient Hebrew books have been found in Palestine from time to time and

A HEBREW ROLL.

the most remarkable finds were made in 1947. These are known as the Dead Sea Scrolls.

A shepherd found the scrolls in a cave near the Dead Sea. They had been wrapped in linen and stored in jars two thousand years ago, a few years before the birth of Christ. Their discovery was of the greatest importance to Bible scholars. Among them was a text of the Book of Isaiah.

"The Book of the Seventy"

Two hundred and fifty years or so before Christ the books of the Hebrew Scriptures began to be translated into Greek, because the King of Egypt at that time wanted to have them in his library at Alexandria. He wanted them in Greek because in those days Egypt was part of the Greek world, and Greek was the language people spoke. This translation is called the "Septuagint" because, according to an ancient legend, the translation was made by seventy Hebrew scholars.

The Greek version, the Septuagint, was copied countless times and used by Greek-speaking Jews. It was in use when Our Lord lived on earth, and as Christianity was spread by the teaching of the Apostles, more and more copies of the Septuagint were made.

Origen's Hexapla

As the centuries passed other Greek translations of the Hebrew Scriptures were made. This was, of course,

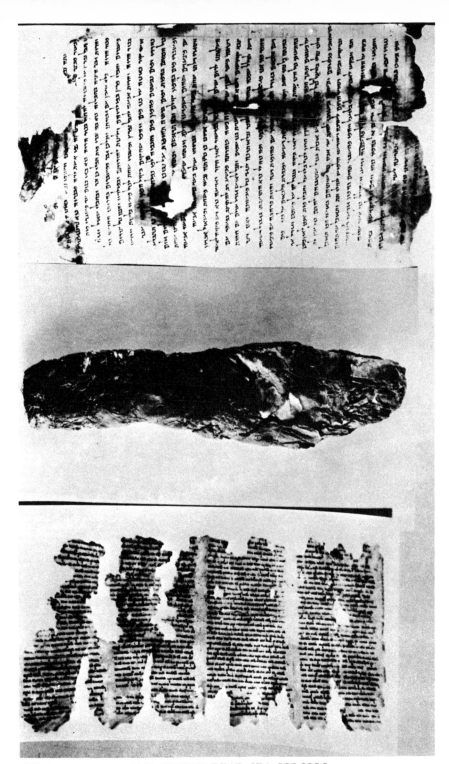

ONE OF THE DEAD SEA SCROLLS.

over a thousand years before the invention of printing, and everything had to be written by hand. With all the copying, mistakes crept in. That is why in the first half of the third century, Origen (A.D. 186-253) made a new version to correct the mistakes.

The Hexapla, as Origen's version was called, has not come down to us complete, but scholars have been able to work out what his famous six-columned book must have looked like.

The Scriptures Jesus Knew

That is the sequence then. First came the Hebrew books, copied many times. They were collected together and translated into Greek about 250 B.C. These were copied in their turn, and Origen collected all the copies he could find and revised them in his Hexapla.

Our English Old Testament is taken directly from the ancient Hebrew versions, so we can read the books of the Old Testament knowing that they have come from the Hebrew Scriptures which Jesus read.

The New Testament Books

The books of the New Testament were written about nineteen hundred years ago in Greek, the language of the eastern Mediterranean lands at that time. It is believed they were all written within a period of about one hundred years. Some were written while men were still alive who had known Jesus Christ and had heard Him teaching. So they are a direct link with Jesus and the early Church.

Many people who lived at the same time as Jesus, or shortly afterward, wrote down their recollections of His teaching. Various writings were in circulation in the early days, some written under the name of an apostle. The different writings often disagreed and the time came when the early Church had to decide which books gave the authentic teaching of Jesus, and discard those which gave only part of it, or a distorted version.

The books which we know in the New Testament are the ones which the Church recognized. They were copied and preserved. Some of the discarded books are known, and one has been rediscovered recently, called the Gospel of Thomas.

As the Apostles traveled about telling people of Jesus and His teaching, the newly converted Christians were naturally eager to read the Gospels and great numbers of copies were made. Often they were written on papyrus. But that does not last long, so it was fortunate for us that they sometimes used vellum, a form of calf-skin, a material that never perishes. A number of early copies of the New Testament books were preserved and it was from them that our New Testament was written.

The Latin Bible

In the time of Jesus nearly all the western world was in the Roman Empire, which stretched from Asia

Minor in the east to Britain in the west. Greek was understood in the east and Latin in the west, and as the first Christian churches were in the east the Bible was written in Greek; but as the Christian faith spread westward, the Bible was translated into Latin.

Christianity continued to spread westward, in spite of the vigorous attempts of the Roman emperors to stamp it out by cruel persecution. Then everything was changed when the Emperor Constantine put an end to the persecution of the Christians in A.D. 313. He made Christianity the religion of the Roman Empire and was himself baptized. As Christianity spread throughout the civilized world of those days, the demand for the Bible became greater than ever. It had to be copied repeatedly, and, careful though the scribes were, mistakes crept in and were multiplied by constant copying.

The Bible of Jerome

The time came when no two Latin Bibles were alike, and the confusion was so great that something had to be done. You read in the story "Jerome the Hermit" how Pope Damasus entrusted Jerome with the task of writing out the Bible anew in A.D. 382. Jerome studied all the different Latin Bibles he could find. He examined the Old Testament books in Hebrew and the New Testament in Greek and in Latin. He compared all the different texts and from his great knowledge he wrote down what seemed to him to be nearest to the original. He worked at the new Bible for fourteen years, first in Rome and then in Bethlehem, in a cave then believed to be next to the place where Jesus was born. Jerome's new Bible was called the Vulgate—from the Latin "Vulgatus," made public or common. It was as correct as Jerome's great scholarship could make it, and it was written in magnificent Latin. The Vulgate was the Bible of the western world for a thousand years, until it was again translated into different languages so that it could be read by people who did not speak Latin.

The books of the Bible were first divided into chapters at the end of the twelfth century by a great Englishman, Stephen Langton, when he was teaching in Paris. Later he became Archbishop of Canterbury. Jewish scribes or scholars divided the Hebrew scriptures into verses not long after the time of Jerome, but the arrangement of the New Testament into verses was the work of a French printer, Robert Estienne, in 1551.

The Oldest Copies of the Bible

Scholars are always striving for the best and purest text of the Bible. The older the document, the nearer it is to the first words written down and the fewer times it will have been copied. For that reason even fragments of really ancient texts on papyrus or vellum are treasured. In certain museums and universities ancient

Bibles and papyrus fragments, in Hebrew and Greek, have been carefully preserved to help scholars in their search for the real meaning of every word in the Bible.

These very old Bibles are called "Codex Vaticanus," or "Codex Sinaiticus," or "Codex Alexandrinus," depending on the place where the manuscript was found or where, as in the case of Codex Vaticanus, it has been housed. The word "codex" is Latin and means tree trunk, but in time it came to be used for wooden leaves or tablets stacked on one another. Thus it was used also to describe sheets of parchment or vellum laid one on another and bound together by sewing. The result was a book not unlike those we read today. By the second and third centuries the codex form of manuscripts had replaced gradually the scroll used for earlier writings.

Codex Vaticanus

As its name tells us, the Codex Vaticanus is in the great Vatican library in Rome. Prepared very early in the fourth century, it is perhaps the most important of the old manuscripts of the Bible, although it is not quite complete. It has suffered from handling so that it contains only 759 of the original 820 leaves. Written by two unknown scribes, it is on very fine vellum. Each leaf measures 10½x10 inches. No one knows how or when it was placed in the Vatican Library but it is known to have been there before 1475.

A MONK COPYING THE PSALMS, ABOUT 1150 (SEE FACING PAGE)

98

SCRIPTOR SCRIPTORVM PRINCEPS EGO NEC OBITVRA DEINCEPS LAVS MEA NEC FAMA QVM

PREDICAT ET OMNINO FAMA PER SECVLA VIGEO · INGENIVM CVIVS LIBRI DECVS IND

CAT HVIVS · QVEM TIBI SEQE DATVM MVNVS DEVS ACCIPE GRATVQ

QM COA LITTERA CLAMAT ETC · TE TVA SCRIPTVRA QVEM SIGNAT PICTA FIGVRA

Codex Sinaiticus

This Bible was written about A.D. 350, or midway in the fourth century. That is, *before* Jerome produced his Latin Bible. The Codex Sinaiticus is a Greek Bible, discovered in most romantic circumstances.

A famous German scholar, Constantine Tischendorf, was traveling in 1844 in search of ancient manuscripts. His travels had brought him to the East, and he was studying old documents in the convent of St. Catherine at the foot of Mount Sinai when he found, in Tischendorf's own words, "in the middle of the great hall a large and wide basket full of old parchments; and the librarian, who was a man of information, told me that two heaps of papers like this, mouldered by time, had been already committed to the flames."

Tischendorf was startled to find among the heap of papers a considerable number of sheets of a copy of the Old Testament in Greek. Since they were to be burned anyway, the monks allowed Tischendorf to take about a third, or forty-three, of the sheets; but because of his apparent excitement and interest, the monks became suspicious as to the value of their possession and would allow the visitor to take no more.

Tischendorf went back to Germany with his great find, but he kept strictly to himself the fact that there was more of the manuscript in the monastery at Mt. Sinai. Nine years later he went back to Sinai and attempted to locate, without arousing the suspicion of the monks, more of the precious sheets. He did not succeed except that in a roll of papers he found a fragment containing eleven short lines from the book of Genesis. To all outward appearances he was simply searching for old manuscripts. He made no mention of the sheets which he had seen previously in the wastebasket, and the monks gave no clue as to what had become of them.

A PAGE OF THE CODEX SINAITICUS, FOURTH CENTURY A.D.

Finally, in 1856, he succeeded in interesting the Czar of Russia in an expedition to locate old and rare manuscripts and so, in 1859, fifteen years after his first discovery, Tischendorf went again to the monastery at the foot of Mount Sinai. This time the trip was financed by the Russian Czar who, unaware of the treasure at Sinai, was interested only in having Tischendorf make an extensive search for valuable documents.

At Sinai, Tischendorf examined old manuscripts but attempted to conceal the fact that he was searching for a particular document. He found no trace of the prized manuscript he was seeking. He was making plans to leave when on his last day he went for a walk with the steward of the monastery. "And as we returned toward sunset he begged me to take some refreshment with him in his cell. Scarcely had he entered the room when, resuming our former subject of conversation, he said, 'And I too have read a Septuagint, a copy of the Greek translation made by the Seventy'; and so saying he took down from the corner of the room a bulky kind of volume wrapped in red cloth. . . ."

At long last Tischendorf held in his hands not only the fragments which fifteen years before he had taken from the basket but also other parts of the Old Testament, the complete New Testament, and some sheets from other very old writings. Taking great care this time not to reveal his excitement, he asked and received permission from the steward to examine the manuscript in his own quarters. Through the night he read, translated, and studied.

But again Tischendorf was not to be allowed to take the manuscript away from the monastery. He asked only to be allowed to take it to Cairo where it could be copied, but the prior of the monastery was away, in Cairo as it happened, attending an election of a new archbishop. No one else had authority to grant Tischendorf the permission he needed.

He made a hurried trip to Cairo to see the prior, who instructed a servant to go immediately by camel to bring the manuscript to Cairo. In nine days Tischendorf had the manuscript in his hands but it was simply a loan. There were more than one hundred and ten thousand lines to be translated and copied; the heat in Cairo was oppressive; and Tischendorf was faced with what seemed an impossible task.

He artfully suggested to the monks at Mt. Sinai that it would be fitting to give the manuscript to the Russian Czar, protector of the Greek Orthodox Church to which the monastery belonged, but months were to pass and many negotiations undertaken before Tischendorf's suggestion became a reality.

In 1933 the British Government purchased from Russia this invaluable manuscript and so, today, much of the Old Testament and all of the New Testament is in the British Museum. The sheets he had found in the wastebasket were presented by Tischendorf himself to the University of Leipzig in Germany, where they were given the name Codex Frederick Augustus in honor of the king of Saxony who had helped with arrangements for Tischendorf's first Eastern trip to search for old manuscripts.

Codex Alexandrinus

Alongside the Codex Sinaiticus in the British Museum is the Codex Alexandrinus, written in the first half of the fifth century, between A.D. 400 and 450. Like the Codex Sinaiticus, it is written in Greek letters on fine vellum and has been bound by modern hands. It was originally a complete Greek Bible, but a number of pages is missing, lost centuries ago.

The Codex Alexandrinus came from Alexandria and found its way to Constantinople, in Turkey. It was presented by the patriarch of Constantinople to James I in 1624, but before it arrived in England the king died. So it was received by Charles I, who was a great lover of art. It remained in the possession of the kings of England until George II presented it to the nation in 1753 when the British Museum was founded.

Other Ancient Manuscripts

France has a famous Greek manuscript, one a little more recent than the Codex Alexandrinus. Housed in the national library in Paris is an early fifth-century manuscript known as Codex Ephraemi-Syri. Originally it contained the entire Bible, but through the years parts have been lost or destroyed. Today there are 209 leaves, measuring 12¼x9½ inches. The pages were used by a scribe in the twelfth century who wrote over the faint letters of the original manuscript, so the precious writing of the fifth century is underneath the writing of the twelfth.

Cambridge University, England, has owned since 1581 a fifth-century manuscript in Greek and Latin. Known as the Codex Bezae, this manuscript contains 406 vellum leaves measuring 10x8 inches. Originally there may have been as many as 510 leaves or more. In this manuscript the Greek and Latin texts face each other on opposite pages, the Greek text on the left and the Latin text on the right.

The Freer Gallery of Art in Washington, D.C., contains Codex Washingtonianus, a fifth-century manuscript of the Gospels. There are 187 leaves, measuring 8⅛x5⅜ inches. This is said to be one of the most important New Testament manuscripts in America, although there are valuable fragments in other museums and libraries.

There are many other old manuscripts, or parts of old manuscripts, containing fragments of the Bible. Very rarely are any two exactly alike. *The Interpreter's Dictionary of the Bible* states, "No other writing which has come to us from the ancient world has had so great an influence upon Western life and culture as the New

Testament. And yet, the text of no other body of ancient literature exists in so many different forms."

And still the scholars continue to search, to study, and to interpret. It is hoped you will share their interest and will want to make your own study.

CHAPTER V

The Bible in English

For more than a thousand years the Bibles used in England were copies of Jerome's Latin Vulgate. It could be read, of course, only by priests and scholars who knew Latin; ordinary people were not able to understand a word of it. The first person we know about who tried to turn parts of the Bible into English was Caedmon, a humble peasant who worked at the Abbey of Whitby about A.D. 670.

The Songs of Caedmon

Caedmon was a shy man who could neither read nor write; he looked after the animals at the Abbey. The story is that one night Caedmon had a vivid dream, in which he recited a long poem about God's creation of the world. He remembered the dream in the morning and told his friends. They took him to the Abbess, who summoned some of the monks and told Caedmon to recite his dream poem. Everyone was astonished at its beauty and it was carefully written down.

Caedmon became a monk and was taught the Scriptures. From time to time Caedmon made up a poem about the Scriptures; it was written down, and in this way he turned many parts of the Bible into English poetry. It was not a true translation, of course; it was a paraphrase, which means that the poem gave the general meaning of the Bible passage.

If we heard Caedmon's poems read aloud we should not understand them, for nowadays Old English can only be understood by scholars. But it was the language used by everyone in England then, and Caedmon is remembered as the first man we know who tried to translate the Bible into English.

Bede, the Monk of Jarrow

Bede went to the monastery of Jarrow in the year 680 when he was seven years old. He was a choir boy at first, but when he grew up he became a monk. He was a great scholar and he wrote more than forty books on religious subjects, all in Latin. But Bede wanted ordinary people to be able to read or hear in English parts of the Bible, so he translated some of it into English, including the Lord's Prayer.

The Lindisfarne Gospels

In the days of Bede the English monasteries were famous throughout the world for the great scholarship of the monks. They were skilled in the arts of writing, painting, sculpture, and needlework. Some of the Latin Bibles copied by the English monks more than a thousand years ago are still treasured in libraries and museums. They wrote beautifully on creamy vellum, and often the first letters of chapters and the margins of the pages were exquisitely painted. For the decoration they painted flowers and trees, birds, animals, and strange monsters, in shades of gold and red, blue and green.

The most famous of these medieval Bibles is the Lindisfarne Gospels. The book was copied and painted about A.D. 690 in the Abbey of Lindisfarne, and treasured by the Abbey. When the Danes invaded England in 875 the monks fled, and took the precious book with them. They tried to escape to Ireland, and the book was dropped into the sea, from which, according to an old legend, it was recovered as a result of a miraculous dream.

The Lindisfarne Gospels are now in the British Museum. The first page of St. Luke's Gospel (see page 110) shows how beautifully the monks worked twelve hunyears ago, and how gay they were too. Imagine what that page looks like as it really is, painted in rich glowing colors!

You will discover many charming little pictures worked into the lovely design. The loop of the big letter Q contains two birds and two long creatures with their tails intertwined, and there are more creatures and birds in the tail of the Q. Eight birds, each holding the legs of the one above, are painted in the right-hand margin, with a cat's head and front legs at the bottom, and his hind legs and a curled-up tail at the top. Perhaps the cat has eaten the birds. In the bottom margin are four more birds.

If you look closely you will see very small words written between the lines. That is an Old English trans-

A PAGE OF THE LINDISFARNE GOSPELS,
THE OPENING OF ST. LUKE'S GOSPEL.

lation written in by a monk who wanted to read the Bible in his own language as well as in Latin.

King Alfred the Great

King Alfred was a great king, a great warrior and a great scholar. He came to the throne of the kingdom of Wessex, the southern part of England, when the heathen Danes had captured and occupied the rest of the land. In 878 Alfred defeated the Danes and, instead of slaying his enemy, he converted him and his followers to Christianity. Slowly the Danes forsook their heathen gods, and learned to live in peace with the English.

With peace established, King Alfred did all he could to make England once again a land of learning and culture. He founded schools and rebuilt the monasteries and he invited scholars to come from abroad to live in England. He set scholars to work translating Latin books into English and he himself may have translated parts of the Bible, including the Ten Commandments, the Law of Moses, and the Psalms.

The First Complete English Bible

From time to time parts of the Bible had been translated into English, but the Bible was not completely written in English until 1382. John Wycliffe was the Rector of Lutterworth, in Leicestershire. He was a great scholar who felt that much was wrong with the Church

111

of his day. He tried to reform it in many ways, and he sent out "poor priests" to travel about the country preaching. Above all, he wanted people to be able to read the Bible in English. Wycliffe has been called the "morning star of the Reformation," the religious revolution which later was to sweep Western Europe and result in the forming of the Protestant Church.

With a few devoted friends Wycliffe translated the whole Bible and a great number of copies were made. As you read in the story "The Bible in English" (page 48) people were eager to hear the Bible in their own language, and the Church tried to stop them. The bishops believed that the Bible could only be understood properly by priests and that it was wrong for ordinary people to read it.

John Wycliffe died in 1384, before he could be punished, but many of the men who had helped him spent many years in prison as a result. Sometimes harsh sentences were given to people caught reading the English Bible, but men and women boldly defied the bishops and risked the punishment. Some people learned whole chapters by heart.

Many copies of Wycliffe's Bible were destroyed, and as the years passed it seemed that his great work was forgotten. But many people in England believed that the Bible should be in English, so that everyone could understand it and read God's message for themselves instead of hearing it only from the priests.

"The New Learning"

In the fifteenth century many Greek scholars came to Italy and brought with them a store of ancient books which had been hidden for centuries in the libraries of Constantinople and other cities. Italian scholars, who had not had the chance to read Greek manuscripts before, learned Greek in order to read them. English and French and German scholars went to Italy and there was great enthusiasm for the "new learning." It was not new really but a revival of interest in the old learning of the ancient world.

Among the manuscripts were some ancient copies in Greek of the books of the Bible. When these were examined scholars realized that the Vulgate, the Church's official Latin Bible, contained many mistakes which had crept in through much copying. This made people want to revise the text of the Bible in order to make it more perfect.

The Invention of Printing

The printing press was invented in the middle of the fifteenth century, and at last there was no need to write books by hand; any number of books could be produced and all would be exactly the same. Johann Gutenberg, a German printer, invented movable type sometime before 1456. The first large work to be set in movable type was the Gutenberg Bible, a printed edition of the Latin Vulgate. About 1516 a Dutch scholar named

Erasmus examined some of the Greek texts, and from them compiled and had printed a New Testament.

William Tyndale's Bible

In "Smugglers' Bible" in Part I (page 60) you read the story of William Tyndale. John Wycliffe's Bibles had all been laboriously copied by hand; Tyndale's translation was printed in thousands. He used the printed Greek New Testament of Erasmus and took the Old Testament from the old Hebrew versions. He could not print it in England, so he worked abroad, and, as you have read, smuggled the Bibles into the country hidden in the cargo of ships.

Tyndale's English Bible was not only the work of a very brave man who gave his life for his beliefs, it was also the work of a very great scholar. Much of the Bible we use today is in his words.

The King Allows the English Bible

Tyndale's last prayer before he was executed was: "Lord, open the King of England's eyes!" It was soon answered, for two years later King Henry VIII ordered that a copy of the Bible in English should be put in every church in the land. Six different versions were printed, all within thirty years of the death of Tyndale.

Coverdale's Bible: 1535

Miles Coverdale had been a close friend of Tyndale and his Bible contained the books of the Old Testament

A CHAINED BIBLE IN LINGFIELD CHURCH, SURREY, ENGLAND

which Tyndale had translated in prison and had not been able to print. Coverdale's magnificent translation of the Psalms is still used in the Book of Common Prayer.

Matthew's Bible: 1537

This was the work of another friend of Tyndale, John Rogers, who used the name Thomas Matthews to conceal his own. Rogers was burned at the stake in the reign of Queen Mary, who was a Roman Catholic.

Taverner's Bible: 1539

Taverner was an Oxford scholar and an expert in Greek. His Bible was a revision of Matthew's Bible.

The Great Bible: 1539

This was the Bible which was put in every church in England at the command of King Henry VIII. It was a very large and handsome book, and people flocked to read it and to hear it read. Only a few people could read in those days, but children and grown-ups learned so that they could read the Bible.

The Geneva Bible: 1557

When Queen Mary I came to the throne in 1553 the English Bible was forbidden again, and only the Latin Vulgate was allowed. Men and women were burned to death because they would not become Roman Catholics and many fled the country. Some scholars who fled to Switzerland worked on another English Bible, trying, as always, to make it nearer the original books. It was known as the Geneva Bible, and was nicknamed "Breeches" Bible because they translated Genesis, chapter 3, verse 7, as "And they sewed fig leaves together and made themselves breeches." In the King James Version and the Revised Standard Version of the Bible the word used is "aprons."

The Bishop's Bible: 1568

Queen Elizabeth I came to the throne in 1558 and control by the Roman Catholics ended. So many different English Bibles were then in use that the Archbishop of Canterbury, Matthew Parker, ordered a new translation to be made, to include the best of all the others and to provide one perfect Bible. The Bishops' Bible was a magnificent work, but it never became as popular as had been intended.

The Douay Bible: 1582 and 1609-10

When Queen Elizabeth I succeeded Queen Mary I, many prominent Roman Catholics fled to France because of persecution, and at Rheims and Douay they produced an English Bible for Roman Catholics, the New Testament of which was published at Rheims in 1582 (the translators of the King James Version made some use of this), and the Old Testament published at Douay in 1609-10. They did not use the then newly dis-

117

covered ancient texts but made their translation from Jerome's Latin Bible. It was difficult to read because they used many words which the ordinary Englishman would not understand. The Douay Bible, as it was called, was revised in later years and is still used by many English-speaking Roman Catholics.

The King James Version: 1611

Just as the Bishops' Bible had been intended to take the place of all the others, so King James I ordered a new revision to be made, to be the one and only Bible in English. The story of this Bible is told in "A Treasury of Most Costly Jewels" (page 73). In England the new Bible, published in 1611, was called the Authorized Version. In the United States it is known as the King James Version of the Bible.

Modern Versions

The Bible of 1611 was written in the language of that time. But words change their meaning as time passes and sometimes phrases which were quite clear to the people of 1611 are difficult to understand now. Scholars have continued to study the ancient Hebrew and Greek versions of the Bible and they know more about them now than did the learned men of 1611.

With the more recent discovery of old manuscripts, and the increase in biblical knowledge, plus the changes in the English language already mentioned, there arose a demand for a revision of the King James Version of the Bible. Revisions were undertaken by a team of English and American scholars. There was published in England in 1881 the Revised Version of the New Testament. The Revised Version of the Old Testament followed in 1885.

While these publications represented a masterpiece of scholarship, they did not include all the recommendations of the American scholars and in 1901 there was issued in the United States the American Standard Version of the Bible. It was widely used in America.

The Westminster Version of the Sacred Scriptures, a modern translation by Roman Catholics from the Greek and Hebrew texts, began to appear in 1913. Since that date there has been a new translation of the Bible from the Latin Vulgate by Monsignor Ronald Knox (New Testament, 1945; Old Testament, 1949) although many English-speaking Roman Catholics still use the Douay Bible. (See last paragraph under *Revised Standard Version of the Bible.*)

Other versions in modern English have been written also by Dr. James Moffatt, Dr. Edgar J. Goodspeed, E. V. Rieu (the Gospels) and J. B. Phillips (the New Testament). (See also *The New English Bible.*)

The Revised Standard Version of the Bible

In 1930 the International Council of Religious Education, an association of the educational boards of forty

of the major Protestant denominations of the United
States and Canada, appointed a committee to study the
English and American revisions of the King James Version of the Bible. It was hoped there might be issued a
new edition of the Bible, incorporating the knowledge
which scholars had gained since 1611—a Bible to cap-
ture in the language of today all the simple, classic
beauty of the King James Version.

The Revised Standard Version of the New Testament was published in 1946. When in 1952 the
Revised Standard Version of the Old Testament was
published, more than twenty years had passed since
the original committee was appointed, and more than
thirty-one scholars had been at work on the revision.
Countless thousands of copies of the Revised Standard
Version of the Bible are used in homes and churches
of the United States and Canada.

In 1965 there was published the Roman Catholic
edition of the Revised Standard Version of the New
Testament. This was issued under the auspices of the
Catholic Biblical Association of Great Britain and contains a preface by the Archbishop of Chicago.

The New English Bible

The latest translation, by a team of scholars under
the general editorship of Dr. C. H. Dodd, is being
sponsored by the principal Christian bodies (other than
the Roman Catholic) of the British Isles. It is called

the New English Bible. The New Testament appeared in 1961. This is not a revision of the King James Version but a completely new translation. The New English Bible attempts to present the meaning of the original Hebrew and Greek as understood by the best modern scholars.

A Look at the Changes

The following verses from the Gospel of Matthew (6:28-33) compare Wycliffe's translation of the year 1380 with Tyndale's version of 1525; with the King James Version of 1611; with the Revised Standard Version of 1946; and with the New English Bible of 1961. The language of Wycliffe and the language of Tyndale may seem strange to us today but in those days the people talked and wrote in the manner of these verses.

Wycliffe's Bible (1380)

And of clothinge what ben ye bisie? biholde ye the lilies of the feld hou thei wexen (grow), thei traueilen (travail) not: nether spynnen, and I seye to you that salomon in al his glorie: was not keuerid (covered) as oon of thes; and if God clothith thus the heye (hay) of the feeld, that to dai is and to morewe is cast in to an ouene: hou myche more ye of litil feith? therefo nyle ye be bisie seynge, what schuln we ete or what schuln we drinke? for hethen men sechen alle these thingis and your fadir woot (knows) that ye han nede to alle these thingis; therfor seke ye first the kyngdom of god and his rightfulnesse: and alle these thingis schuln be cast to you.

(From Purvey's revision of the Wycliffe Bible.)

Tyndale's Bible (1525)

And why care ye then for rayment? Consydre the lylies of the felde, how they growe. They labour not neither spynne. And yet for all that I saye unto you, that even Salomon in all his royalte was not arayed lyke unto one of these. Wherfore yf God so clothe the grasse, which ys to daye in the felde, and tomorowe shalbe caste into the fournace, shall he not moche more do the same unto you, o ye of lytle fayth? Therefore take no thought sayinge: what shall we eate, or what shall we drinke, or wherwith shall we be clothed? After all these thinges seke the gentyls. For youre hevenly father knoweth that ye have neade of all these thynges. But rather seke ye fyrst the kyngdome of heven and the rightewisnes thereof, and all these thinges shalbe ministred unto you.

The King James Version of the Bible (1611)

And why take ye thought for rainment? Consider the lilies of the field, how they grow; they toil not, neither do they spin: and yet I say unto you, That even Solomon in all his glory was not arayed like one of these. Wherefore, if God so clothe the grass of the field, which today is, and tomorrow is cast into the oven, *shall he* not much more *clothe* you, O ye of little faith? Therefore take no thought, saying, What shall we eat? or, What shall we drink? or, Wherewithal shall we be clothed? (For all these *things* do the Gentiles seek): for your heavenly Father knoweth that ye have need of all these things. But seek ye first the kingdom of God, and his righteousness; and all these *things* shall be added unto you.

The Revised Standard Version of the Bible (1946)

And why are you anxious about clothing? Consider the lilies of the field, how they grow; they neither toil nor spin; yet I tell you, even Solomon in all his glory was not arrayed like one of these. But if God so clothes the grass of the field, which today is alive and tomorrow is thrown into the oven, will he not much more clothe you, O men of little faith? Therefore do not be anxious, saying, "What shall we eat?" or "What shall we drink?" or "What shall we wear?" For the Gentiles seek all these things; and your heavenly Father knows that you need them all. But seek first his kingdom and his righteousness, and all these things shall be yours as well.

The New English Bible (1961)

And why be anxious about clothes? Consider how the lilies grow in the fields; they do not work, they do not spin; and yet, I tell you, even Solomon in all his splendour was not attired like one of these. But if that is how God clothes the grass in the fields, which is there today and tomorrow is thrown on the stove, will he not all the more clothe you? How little faith you have! No, do not ask anxiously, "What are we going to eat? What are we to drink? What shall we wear?" All these are things for the heathen to run after, not for you, because your heavenly Father knows that you need them all. Set your mind on God's kingdom and his justice before everything else, and all the rest will come to you as well.

Thus, in the middle of the twentieth century scholars are still striving, as did Wycliffe and Tyndale, to provide us with a Bible in English as close as possible to the original Hebrew of the Old Testament and to the Greek of the New Testament.

CHAPTER VI

Digging for Bible History

A great deal has been learned about the Bible from the work of archaeologists, who dig carefully into the ground where once stood ancient cities, temples, or palaces. From their study of such things as broken pottery, fragments of stone, and metal, they are able to find out about the distant past. Sometimes they find evidence directly connected with the Bible.

Many books have been written on this fascinating subject, which is much too large to be dealt with in this book. Two examples, however, will show how the work of the archaeologists can bring the ancient days, forgotten except for the Bible, back to life.

The first example is the excavations which were made on the site of the city of Ur, the home of Abraham. Ur was in Chaldea, east of Palestine across the Arabian Desert. The archaeologists found a number of exquisite objects of gold which showed that once, in the far-off dawn of history, a rich civilization flourished there. They also found something else, a bed of clean silt, or soil deposited by water.

Below the silt they found the ruins of houses which seemed to have been overwhelmed by a flood. They measured the silt and decided that since it was eleven feet deep the water must have been from twenty to twenty-five feet deep. It was clear that if the water was as deep as that it must have covered everything for a

125

GOLD RAM CAUGHT IN A
THICKET, FOUND ON THE
SITE OF THE ANCIENT
CITY OF UR.

hundred square miles between the rivers Tigris and Euphrates.

To the people living there it would have seemed that the whole earth was flooded. That may well have been the origin of the story of the great flood told in the Book of Genesis and in Babylonian myths.

The second example of how the archaeologists discover Bible history in the ground was the excavation of a tunnel cut through the rock on which Jerusalem stands. They found an inscription which proved that the tunnel was made in the time of Hezekiah for taking water into the city if it was besieged. This amazing engineering feat is referred to in the Bible, in II Kings, chapter 20, verse 20.

These two examples show how archaeologists use their knowledge and skill to find out about the days of long ago and increase our knowledge of Bible history.

Skilled men can unravel the secrets of ancient documents, too, often using science to help them. They can read obscure writing on clay tablets, papyrus or parchment, even when they have only torn scraps. The famous Dead Sea Scrolls are an example of this kind of work. They have been pieced together, studied, and translated. When that was done it was seen that these ancient scrolls were a proof of the careful way the books of the Bible had been copied. They showed how near our own Bible is to the original books, written thousands of years ago.

THIS PICTURE IS FROM AN ELEVENTH CENTURY ENGLISH BIBLE. THE BOY ISAAC
IS BEING TAKEN BY HIS FATHER, ABRAHAM, TO BE SACRIFICED.

PART III

The Bible

In part I of this book you have read stories about the Bible. Part II has given some of the known facts about the Bible, describing its long journey from ancient days to the Book we know.

And now, in Part III, we have come to today's Bible. We know that the sixty-six books which make up the Old and New Testaments have a common theme, the story of the coming of the Christ or Messiah. We know that our Old Testament is taken from the Hebrew versions which Jesus read; that the New Testament is based on the writings of men who loved God and were dedicated to the task of discovering and revealing his way of life to all mankind; and we know that most of the books of the New Testament were written while men were still alive who had known Jesus and had heard him teaching.

The pages to follow describe the Bible.

CHAPTER I

The Books of the Bible

It is easier to know and understand the different books of the Bible if you group them together into eight sets; four in the Old Testament and four in the New. This is how you can do it.

The Old Testament

Group I—Five books: *The Creation of the World and the Law*

Genesis	Leviticus	Numbers
Exodus		Deuteronomy

These five books tell the story of the creation of the Universe and of man, the choice of the Jews as God's chosen people, and the giving of the Law by God to Moses.

Group 2—Twelve books: *The History of the Hebrew Nation*

Joshua	II Samuel	II Chronicles
Judges	I Kings	Ezra
Ruth	II Kings	Nehemiah
I Samuel	I Chronicles	Esther

The history of the Hebrew nation, the Jews, for a thousand years is given in these twelve books.

Group 3—Six books: *The Books of Poetry and Wisdom*

Job	Proverbs	The Song of Solomon
The Psalms	Ecclesiastes	Lamentations

Here we have the sacred poetry of the ancient Jews, and collections of wise sayings and proverbs.

Group 4—Sixteen books: *The Books of Prophecy*

Isaiah	Hosea	Nahum
Jeremiah	Joel	Habakkuk
Ezekiel	Amos	Zephaniah
Daniel	Obadiah	Haggai
	Jonah	Zechariah
	Micah	Malachi

The books of prophecy and wisdom of the Hebrews are the writings of their wise men. They were good men, inspired to warn the Jews when they were wrong, often foretelling disasters to come if they did not mend their ways, and sometimes telling of the coming of the Messiah. The books can be divided again into three groups, the major prophets, Isaiah, Jeremiah and Ezekiel; the Book of Daniel which stands apart from the others; and the twelve minor prophets.

The New Testament

Group 1—Five books: *The History of Christ and the Church*

The Gospel According to Matthew
The Gospel According to Mark
The Gospel According to Luke
The Gospel According to John
The Acts of the Apostles

The Gospels were written by four different people, but they all tell the same story, the life, the teaching, the death, and the resurrection of Jesus Christ. The Acts of the Apostles tells us about the Apostles who carried Jesus' teaching abroad and founded the Christian Church.

Group 2—Thirteen books: *Letters of Paul*

Letter to the Romans	I Thessalonians
I Corinthians	II Thessalonians
II Corinthians	I Timothy
Galatians	II Timothy
Ephesians	Titus
Philippians	Philemon
Colossians	

These letters which were written to the newly formed Christian churches are full of advice and encouragement, and have been a guide to Christians ever since. Some scholars think the letters to Timothy and Titus were written by someone other than Paul, perhaps written many years later by someone trying to show what Paul would have advised young ministers.

Group 3—Eight books: *Letters of Other Apostles*

To the Hebrews	I John
James	II John
I Peter	III John
II Peter	Jude

We learn more about the early Church from these letters, and see the problems which faced the first Christians. As with the letters of Paul, these letters are a guide to Christians today just as they were nearly two thousand years ago.

Group 4—One book: *A Book of Prophecy*

The Revelation of John

This book is a vision which looks forward to the final victory of Christianity, the triumph of God over evil.

CHAPTER II

The Contents of the Books of the Bible

It would take many pages to give the contents of every book of the Bible in detail, and there is no "short cut" to knowing the Bible. The only way is to read it. The following notes will tell you in very general terms what the books are about, and where you can find some of the famous stories.

The Old Testament

Group 1: *The Creation of the World and the Law*

Genesis: The word "genesis" means *beginning*. It is the beginning of the Bible and tells the story, as written by the ancient Hebrews, of the beginning of the world. In it we read of the creation of the universe and of man and how the Hebrew nation was made from the ten tribes of Israel.

Exodus: Exodus means *going out*, and the book relates how Moses led the Children of Israel out from slavery under the Egyptians into the wilderness. In the second part of Exodus Moses gives them God's law.

Leviticus: The Levites were the priestly tribe of the Hebrews. Here you can read about their religious rites and customs.

Numbers: The name comes from the "numbering of the people," or the recording of the census. The first section of this book records the size of different tribes and includes other statistical information. The Hebrews wandered homeless in the wilderness for forty years, and in that time they were counted twice.

Deuteronomy: Moses gives the law again and adds to it. The book ends with the death of Moses.

134

Group 2: *The History of the Hebrew Nation*

Joshua: After Moses, Joshua was the great leader of the Children of Israel. It was he who led them into Canaan, "the Promised Land," after Moses died. It is the story of the conquest of the Promised Land.

Judges: After Joshua died the Hebrews were ruled by "Judges." The book continues the story of the conquest of Canaan.

Ruth: One of the shortest books, containing only four chapters. It is a very beautiful story of Ruth, ancestress of David.

I Samuel: The history of the Hebrews in the days of Samuel, the prophet, and afterward. The book has many famous stories, especially of Samuel, Saul, and David.

II Samuel: The reign of the great King David. The writing of the two books of Samuel began nearly a thousand years before Christ.

I Kings: The history of the reign of King Solomon and of the division of the land into two kingdoms, the northern one called Israel and the southern called Judah. The period covered is from 970 to 842 B.C.

II Kings: The history of the two kingdoms is continued to the fall of the northern kingdom in 722 B.C. and to the fall of the southern kingdom and the destruction of Jerusalem, the capital, in 586 B.C. The Children of Israel are taken away as captives to the land of Babylon.

I Chronicles: The two books of Chronicles are repetitions of the history told in the books of Samuel and Kings. The events are seen, however, from the point of view of the priests. The main story in I Chronicles is about David.

II Chronicles: The incidents already told in the books of Kings are retold in another way: the reign of Solomon, the building of the great Temple at Jerusalem, and, after Solomon's death, the history of the other kings who followed him, down to the destruction of Jerusalem and the captivity in Babylon.

Ezra: The book of Ezra tells of the return of some of the captive Jews from Babylon. It is named after Ezra, the priest who went back to Jerusalem from Babylon with some of the Hebrews. It tells also of the rebuilding of the Temple in Jerusalem.

Nehemiah: The principal event in the book of Nehemiah is the building of the walls of Jerusalem. It also gives the history of the people after the return from Babylon until the year 432 B.C. Nehemiah reformed the religious customs.

Esther: The book of Esther was written about 150 B.C. and is one of the latest books of the Old Testament. It is an exciting and beautiful story of the Jewess, Esther, who became Queen of Persia.

Group 3: *The Books of Poetry, including the Books of Wise Sayings, or Wisdom Books*

Job: The book of Job is really a play. God, Satan, and Job are the main characters. It is a religious discussion, in which Job complains bitterly of his sufferings. In the end he recovers his belief in God.

The Psalms: This might be called the Hebrew hymnbook. It is a wonderful collection of hymns of praise to God. They were written over a period of a thousand years or more, and the earliest are believed to have been written by David.

Proverbs: A collection of wise sayings; some of them were attributed to King Solomon.

Ecclesiastes: Another book of wisdom. The writer is unknown.

The Song of Solomon: A beautiful love poem, which is also called "The Song of Songs," supposed in ancient times to have been written by King Solomon.

Lamentations: A short book which was ascribed to Jeremiah in ancient times. It is a collection of sad poems written after Jerusalem had been captured.

Group 4: *The Books of Prophecy*

Isaiah: Isaiah comes first in the seventeen books of prophecy in the Old Testament, and it is considered to be the greatest of them all. Isaiah prophesied in Jerusalem between 740 and 701 B.C., but the book includes the words of other prophets who lived after him. The writings of one of these, in chapters 40 to 55, are of the greatest importance. The prophet writes a poem about the "Servant of the Lord," who recalls the nations to God at the cost of his own suffering and death. It is a vision which foretells the coming of Jesus Christ.

Jeremiah: Jeremiah lived in the period just before the Jews were taken into exile in Babylon. He was often in prison and often punished, but he had unconquerable courage and never hesitated to say what he knew was right.

Ezekiel: Ezekiel heartened the Hebrews during their exile in Babylon by foretelling their return to their own land and the rebuilding of Jerusalem and the Temple, prophecies which came true.

Daniel: The book of Daniel is full of stirring stories. Those of Shadrach, Meshach, and Abednego in the fiery furnace and of Daniel in the lions' den are among the best known in the Bible.

Hosea: This is the first of the twelve books of the "minor" prophets. Hosea was a prophet a hundred and fifty years earlier than Ezekiel. He belongs to the northern kingdom of the two into which Palestine was divided.

Joel: A short book of prophecy threatening disaster if the Jews did not reform their ways and obey the Law. Joel wrote because a terrible plague of locusts threatened the land with famine.

Amos: Amos was a simple herdsman who prophesied between 760 and 750 B.C. He was the earliest of the prophets whose writings would be made into a book. He taught that God is just and fair and demands fair dealing in daily life.

Obadiah: With one chapter only, this is the shortest book in the Old Testament. Obadiah lived in the early years of exile in Babylon, and he reproached the neighboring nation of Edom for not helping the Jews in their struggle with Babylon.

Jonah: A magnificent story which shows the duty of Israel to bring the Gentiles, or non-Hebrew peoples, to God. In the story Jonah has various adventures, including the famous one of being swallowed by a giant fish.

Micah: Micah lived at the same time as Isaiah, a time of war. This book contains a prophecy that one day peace would come to all the world, through the mercy of God, and that the Messiah would be born in Bethlehem.

Nahum: A poem about the fall of Assyria, the hated enemy of the Hebrews, and its capital the city of Nineveh, in 612 B.C.

Habakkuk: Habakkuk lived a few years after Nahum. He asks if the good really prosper and the evil suffer, and shows that this is so. He foretells the ultimate delivery of the Hebrews from their suffering at the hands of their many enemies.

Zephaniah: Written about the same time as the books of Nahum and Habakkuk, this prophecy sharply criticizes the Jews for worshiping the false god Baal. It is a sad, solemn book.

Haggai: The book of Haggai has only two chapters. Haggai was the first prophet to write after the return of the Hebrews from Babylon, and he encourages them to make a new start and to rebuild the Temple.

Zechariah: Zechariah, who lived at the same time as Haggai, also tried to awaken the Hebrews to make a new beginning as a nation.

Malachi: The last book of the Old Testament looks forward to the New Testament. Malachi blames the priests for being lazy, and promises the coming of a messenger, the forerunner of the Messiah. *Malachi* means "my messenger."

The New Testament

Group 1: *The Gospels and the Acts*

The word "gospel" means *good tidings.* The four Gospels, by Matthew, Mark, Luke, and John, all tell the story of the life and teaching of Jesus. The differences are in the way in which the stories are told, and in the details.

Matthew: Matthew wrote his Gospel to be read by the Hebrews, Jesus' own nation. He shows how the coming of Jesus was foretold in the Hebrew Scriptures, the Old Testament. This Gospel tells us most fully what Jesus taught in the Sermon on the Mount and in His parables and short sayings.

Mark: The Gospel of Mark was probably written before the others. There is a tradition dating back to the earliest Christian times that when Mark wrote his gospel he based it on his memories of what Peter had told him about Jesus. Another writer has said he wrote after Peter's death. There are still other traditions and we cannot be sure about it.

Luke: Luke was a doctor. His Gospel was written to be read by the Gentiles, the non-Jewish people. Luke tells how Jesus came to redeem all mankind and not only the Jews.

John: John's Gospel was written after the other three. It does not so much tell the story of Jesus' life as explain its deeper meaning.

The Acts of the Apostles: Written by Luke as the sequel to his gospel, the Acts of the Apostles gives the history of the early Church, up to A.D. 62. You can read in the second chapter how, on the day of Pentecost, the Holy Spirit descended on the disciples. The Acts tell how the Apostles traveled about the world spreading the gospel, and how the small Christian communities were formed which became the Christian Church. Paul is the hero of the later chapters.

Group 2: *The Letters of Paul*

Romans: This letter was written in Corinth in A.D. 56. It was sent to the Christian converts in Rome, telling them that Paul was going to visit them and explaining the Christian faith and way of life.

I Corinthians: The members of the Church in Corinth, a great trading center for both east and west, had sent Paul a list of questions about their new religion. Paul replies in this fine letter and tells them how to live as true Christians among the temptations of the city.

II Corinthians: In this letter to the Christians in Corinth, written in the same year as the first one, Paul tells how pleased he is with good news he has received from them, advises them, and arranges for a collection to help Christians in Palestine.

Galatians: Writing to the Christians in Galatia, a Roman province in Asia Minor, Paul explains that the Law of Moses, in the Hebrew Scriptures, was a preparation for Christ, whom they must trust and obey.

Ephesians: A letter from Paul, written when he was in prison in Rome, or perhaps by someone else writing for Paul. Although the letter is addressed to the Ephesians it was probably a "circular letter," taken by a messenger from church to church in Asia Minor. The letter reminds Christians that Christ's message is not only for the Jews but for all mankind.

Philippians: Written from prison in Rome to the Christians at Philippi in Macedonia.

Colossians: Writing from prison to the Christians at Colossae in

Phrygia, Paul reminds them that they must not follow the old Jewish religious customs, mixed with heathen beliefs, such as belief in the influence of stars, which were dangerously popular in Asia Minor.

I Thessalonians: Paul praises the Christians at Thessalonica, in Macedonia, for remaining constant under persecution.

II Thessalonians: More encouragement to the Christians at Thessalonica to withstand the persecution by the Romans and to trust in God, however cruelly they suffer.

I Timothy: Paul advises Timothy, head of the church at Ephesus, how to manage his church. Many think the letters to Timothy and Titus were written many years later by someone trying to show what Paul would have advised young ministers of that time.

II Timothy: A letter describing Paul's second imprisonment, when he knew that he would soon be killed.

Titus: Paul advises Titus, head of the church in Crete, how to manage his church.

Philemon: A private letter written by Paul to help a converted Christian, Onesimus. Onesimus was a slave who had robbed his master, a rich Christian in Laodicea, and had run away. Paul sent the slave back to his master to ask forgiveness and and gave him this letter to take with him.

Group 3: *Letters Written by Other Apostles*

Hebrews: This letter was probably addressed to Jewish Christians. It tells them that when they become Christian they must move on beyond the religious customs of their old faith. People used to think that Paul wrote it, but now it is known that he did not. The author is unknown.

James: Addressed to all Christians, this is more a sermon than a letter. We do not know who James was, but he may have been a brother of Jesus.

I Peter: Another letter to encourage Christians to be faithful in spite of the cruel persecution they suffered.

II Peter: A general letter to the early Christians, warning them against false teaching.

I John: It is believed that this letter was written by the same man who wrote the Gospel of John. It urges all Christians to be brothers in the faith of Christ.

II John: The subject of this letter is the same as the previous one —brotherly love.

III John: A letter written to an individual emphasizing the importance of brotherly love and the Christian faith.

Jude: A letter which warns Christians to ignore false teachers.

Group 4: *A Book of Prophecy*

Revelation to John: The last book in the New Testament was written when Christians were being cruelly persecuted by the Romans. It is full of strange visions and looks forward to the time when good will overcome evil and Christ will reign in triumph. It is written in such a way that only Christians could understand its true meaning.

The Apocrypha

The Bible has three sections: the Old and New Testaments, and the Apocrypha, which has fourteen books. The Hebrews did not consider these books sacred, so they left them out of their Scriptures. They were included in the ancient Greek version of the Bible, as part of the Old Testament, and St. Jerome put them in his Latin Bible, the Vulgate.

But when the Bible was translated into English in

CHAPTER III

Stories in the Bible

The Bible is called the Word of God, because it is the book in which God reveals himself to mankind. The Gospels in the New Testament are the source of our knowledge of the teaching of Jesus Christ on which the Christian faith is built. You will see, therefore, that the Bible is the greatest book in the world, and very much more than a storybook.

Yet the Bible is full of wonderful stories, which have been loved by children of many races for two thousand years and which have shown men and women through the ages how to live. They are tales of ancient peoples living a very different life from ours today.

You are missing a good deal if you do not read the Bible often. The pleasure is two-fold: in the stories themselves and in the splendor of the language. If you are in a room alone, read aloud, or if not, read aloud in your head. Then you will "hear" the music of the language and understand its beauty.

It is a good idea to act some of the stories. Three or four of you can take a part each and read your speeches, or, better still, learn them by heart. You can make the words into speeches with a little thought. Another way is to put the speeches into your own words.

The following list tells you where you can find some of the most famous stories. Remember, they have been known by children for two thousand years.

Stories from the Old Testament

The Creation

Genesis, chapters 1 and 2

"In the beginning God created the heaven and the earth." These are the first words in the Bible, and the first chapter of Genesis tells the biblical story of the beginning of all things. It tells how God created light, heaven, the earth, and the sea; the plants and flowers; the seasons, the sun, moon, and stars; fish, birds, and animals and, finally, man.

Adam and Eve

Genesis, chapters 2 and 3

The story of Adam and Eve, in the Garden of Eden, and how they ate the forbidden fruit and were driven out of the garden.

Noah's Ark

Genesis, chapter 6, verse 13, to chapter 8, verse 22

Mankind has become sinful and God decides to drown the earth with a great flood. One good man, Noah, is warned of the calamity and told to build an ark, or a ship. In this he takes his family and two each of every animal and bird. So mankind and the birds and beasts are preserved, to make a new start.

Abraham and Isaac

Genesis, chapter 22, verses 1 to 13

God tests Abraham by telling him to take his own son, Isaac, to a mountain to kill him as an offering to God. Abraham does as he is commanded, grieving deeply, and prepares to slay his much loved son. At the last minute God saves Isaac.

Jacob's Dream

Genesis, chapter 28, verses 10 to 22

The story of a wonderful dream which came to Jacob, Abraham's grandson and the ancestor of the Children of Israel.

Joseph Sold as a Slave by His Brothers
Genesis, chapter 37, verses 5 to 36
Joseph, one of the brothers of Jacob, had two dreams which he tells to his brothers. They are so angry that they want to kill him, but they change their minds and sell him as a slave to some Egyptians.

Joseph and Pharaoh
Genesis, chapter 41, verses 1 to 45
Joseph interprets a strange dream for Pharaoh and becomes the highest official in all Egypt.

Joseph and His Brothers
Genesis, chapter 42, verse 3, to chapter 45, verse 15
Joseph's ten brothers go to Egypt to buy corn, for there is a famine in their land. They do not recognize in the great prince the brother they once sold as a slave. The story tells how pleased Joseph is to see them aagin, but how he teases them before he makes himself known.

Moses in the Bulrushes
Exodus, chapter 2, verses 2 to 10
The cruel King of Egypt orders that every baby boy born to the Hebrews must be thrown into the Nile. To save his life, one baby is put into a cradle of rushes and hidden among the reeds on the bank of the Nile while his sister watches, in the hope that some Egyptian will save him. It so happens that the King's daughter finds him. She adopts him, calls him Moses, and brings him up as a prince.

Moses and the Burning Bush
Exodus, chapter 3, verses 1 to 9
Moses is tending a flock of sheep when he sees a burning bush

and hears God telling him of his plan to have Moses lead the oppressed Israelites out of Egypt.

Moses and the Israelites Cross the Red Sea
Exodus, chapter 14, verses 1 to 30
Under God's direction Moses leads the people of Israel across the Red Sea.

The Ten Commandments
Exodus, chapter 20, verses 2 to 17
Moses grows up and becomes the leader of the Hebrews. He takes the Hebrews out of slavery in Egypt to freedom, for God has promised to guide him to a land flowing with "milk and honey." While they are traveling in the wilderness, God calls Moses to a mountaintop and gives him the Ten Commandments.

Samuel Is Called by God
I Samuel, chapter 3, verses 1 to 20
The boy Samuel is taken to the Temple by his mother and becomes the servant of the priest Eli. God speaks to Samuel, and Eli realizes that the boy is to become a great prophet.

David Chosen to Be King
I Samuel, chapter 16
Samuel is told by God to anoint a youth named David to become King in place of King Saul, who has displeased God. David goes to the Palace to soothe King Saul by playing his harp.

David and the Giant
I Samuel, chapter 17
In a war between Israel and the Philistines, a giant named Goliath comes forward to challenge any Israelite to individual combat. None dares to confront the mighty Goliath, until David, a young

shepherd boy, accepts the challenge. He faces Goliath armed only
with a sling, slays the giant, and wins favor with King Saul.

David Spares Saul's Life

I Samuel, chapter 26, verses 7 to 25

David incurred the enmity of Saul, and Saul pursued him relent-
lessly. To prove that Saul need have no fear of him, David stole
into the king's camp and took his spear and water jug but did
not harm Saul.

Solomon and the Two Mothers

1 Kings, chapter 3, verses 16 to 28

Solomon is famous for his great wisdom. Two mothers are brought
to him, quarreling because each claims to be the mother of a baby.
Solomon finds out which is the baby's mother by a clever method.

Elijah and the Ravens

I Kings, chapter 17

The prophet Elijah has to hide in the mountains during a time
of persecution. He is fed by the ravens who bring him food in their
beaks. When the little stream from which he drinks dries up he
goes to the house of a poor woman and miraculously obtains food
and drink. The woman's son dies and Elijah restores him to life.

The Three Young Men

Daniel, chapter 3, verses 8 to 30

Three young men, Shadrach, Meshach and Abednego, refuse to
obey King Nebuchadnezzar when he orders everyone to worship a
golden image. Because of their defiance they are thrown into the
fiery furnace, but they survive.

Daniel in the Lions' Den

Daniel, chapter 6, verses 1 to 24

The prophet Daniel is made the first man in the kingdom, and the other princes are jealous. To trick Daniel, they persuade the King, Darius, to pass a decree that anyone who makes any petition or prays to anyone but the King for thirty days shall be thrown into the lions' den. Daniel prays to God three times a day, as he always does, so he is thrown into the lions' den, but the lions do not harm him.

Stories from the New Testament

The Gospels

The Gospels in the New Testament are, of course, the most wonderful stories of all, for they tell of the life of Jesus Christ.

The Birth of Jesus
Luke, chapter 2, verses 1 to 20
This is the lovely story we know so well from our Christmas services and carols, the humble beginning of the life of Jesus. The story is told also in Matthew, chapter 2, verses 1 to 12.

Jesus Visits the Temple
Luke, chapter 2, verses 40 to 52
Here we read how Jesus grows up and how, when He is twelve, He is lost in Jerusalem and found in the Temple, talking with the priests.

The Temptation of Jesus
Matthew, chapter 4, verses 1 to 11
Jesus is baptized by John the Baptist and then goes into the wilderness, fasting for forty days. When He is weak with hunger He is tempted to use His power as the Son of God for His own benefit.

The First Disciples

Mark, chapter 1, verses 14 to 20

Jesus calls His first disciples to Him. They are simple fishermen on the Sea of Galilee, who leave everything to follow Him.

The Sermon on the Mount

Matthew, chapters 5, 6, and 7

The message of Jesus to mankind, given as nearly as we can tell in His own words. These three chapters contain the new ideas which changed the world.

Christ's Death and Resurrection

All four Gospels, Matthew, Mark, Luke, and John, give this glorious story. The end of Christ's life on earth was the beginning of the Christian faith. It is the most important part of the whole Bible.

The Acts of the Apostles

The First Christian Martyr

Acts, chapter 7, verses 54 to 60

Countless men and women have died for the Christian Faith. The first of the martyrs was Stephen. You will find that a young man named Saul is mentioned; he became Paul, the leader of the early Christians.

Saul Is Converted

Acts, chapter 9, verses 11 to 22

Saul, the clever lawyer and the leader of the persecution of the Christians, is traveling towards Damascus when he has an amazing experience and becomes a new man. He changes his name and is known to us as Paul.

Paul on Trial

  Acts, chapters 25 and 26

  Paul is now brought to trial himself for being a Christian and
  answers his judges with great spirit. Being a Roman citizen, he
  appeals to the emperor in Rome.

Paul Is Shipwrecked

  Acts, chapter 27 to chapter 28, verse 10

  Paul is sent from Palestine to Rome to be tried. He embarks on
  a ship with other prisoners, and there follows an account of a
  most adventurous voyage, the ship running before a gale, going
  aground and eventually being wrecked off Melita, or Malta as we
  now call it. It is largely owing to Paul's God-sent wisdom that all
  are saved. This is a thrilling sea story. The scene of the shipwreck
  is now known as St. Paul's Bay and a statue of the apostle stands
  at the entrance to it.

Paul's Letters

These are not really stories, but they are wonderful
reading. You will notice Paul's strong manly way of
writing, and his simplicity of thought. These three
pieces are good samples of his letters. They are better
read aloud or aloud in your head.

Brotherly Love

  Romans, chapter 12, verses 10 to 21

  Paul tells us to carry out Christ's teaching by being kind, forgiving
  our enemies, and living peaceably with each other.

Be Charitable

  I Corinthians, chapter 13, verses 1 to 13

This is one of the most famous passages in all Paul's writing; it is splendid read aloud and slowly.

The Peace of God
Philippians, chapter 4, verses 4 to 8
Another very great passage which has great wisdom matched with great words, and another passage to read aloud for its music.

BOOKS ABOUT THE BIBLE

THERE ARE VERY MANY BOOKS ABOUT THE BIBLE; HERE ARE A FEW
YOU WILL PROBABLY BE ABLE TO GET FROM YOUR PUBLIC LIBRARY.
FINDING OUT ABOUT THE BIBLE IS A FASCINATING HOBBY, WHICH GROWS
IN INTEREST AS YOU DISCOVER MORE ABOUT THE SUBJECT. IT IS A GOOD
IDEA TO START A SCRAPBOOK FOR PICTURES AND ARTICLES YOU CUT OUT
FROM NEWSPAPERS AND MAGAZINES. BUT REMEMBER, THE BEST WAY
TO DISCOVER THE BIBLE IS TO READ IT.

THE BIBLE

The Young Readers Bible. 1965. Published by A. J. Holman &
    Company for distribution through Cokesbury Book Store.
The Revised Standard Version of the Bible.
The New English Bible.
The King James Version of the Bible.

THE MAKING OF THE BIBLE

Jones, Mary Alice. Know Your Bible. Rand-McNally, 1965.
Kelsey, Alice Geer. Adventures With the Bible. Friendship Press,
    1960.

Klaperman, Gilbert. *The How and Why Wonder Book of the Old Testament.* Grosset & Dunlap Company, 1965.

Oliver, Jane. *Watch for the Morning.* St. Martin's Press, 1964.

TO HELP YOU READ THE BIBLE

Ferrien, Samuel. *The Golden Bible Atlas.* Golden Press, 1960.

Northcott, Cecil. *Bible Encyclopedia for Children.* Westminster Press, 1964.

Smither, Ethel L. *A Picture Book of Palestine.* Abingdon Press, 1947.

Tubby, Ruth. *A Picture Dictionary of the Bible.* Abingdon Press, 1949.

Honour, Alan. *Cave of Riches: The Story of the Dead Sea Scrolls.* McGraw-Hill, 1956.

Bouquet, A. C. *Everyday Life in New Testament Times.* Charles Scribner's Sons, 1954.

Heaton, E. W. *Everyday Life in Old Testament Times.* Charles Scribner's Sons, 1956.

STORIES RETOLD FROM THE BIBLE

Bowie, Walter Russell. *The Bible Story for Boys and Girls: New Testament.* Abingdon Press, 1951.

Bowie, Walter Russell. *The Bible Story for Boys and Girls: Old Testament.* Abingdon Press, 1952.

Doss, Helen. *Jonah.* Abingdon Press, 1964.

Bowie, Walter Russell. *The Story of the Bible.* Abingdon Press, 1934.

Fosdick, Harry Emerson. *Jesus of Nazareth.* Random House, 1959.

Hogan, Bernice. *Deborah.* Abingdon Press, 1964.

Jones, Mary Alice. *Bible Stories.* Rand-McNally Company, 1952.

Meyer, Edith P. *The Three Guardsmen and Other Stories from the Apocrypha.* Abingdon Press, 1960.

Notes on the Photographs

Facing page 90—The Hebrew Scriptures used in the synagogues were mounted on rollers. As the priest read, he unrolled with one hand and wound the strip on to the other roller with the other hand. This roll is 19 inches high and many feet in length.

Facing page 92—A page of the Book of Isaiah, discovered in 1947 with many other ancient scrolls in a cave near the Dead Sea. Written on leather 2,000 years ago, it is 10 inches high and 24 feet long. The roll is shown in the center, as it was found, wrapped in linen.

Facing page 98—This picture is from a book of the Psalms written in Canterbury about the year 1150 and known as the Eadwine Psalter or Canterbury Psalter. The picture is a portrait of the monk Eadwine and shows him carefully writing. In his right hand he holds a pen; in his left hand is a knife for scraping the vellum clean if he makes a mistake.

Facing page 100—A page from the Codex Sinaiticus, so called because codex means pages of writing bound as a book and these pages were found in a monastery on Mount Sinai. It was written in Greek in the middle of the fourth century A.D. on very fine vellum, which is prepared from skins of calves, or lambs. It is one of the great treasures of the British Museum.

Facing page 111—A page from the Lindisfarne Gospels, written and illuminated by an English monk about the year 690. Notice the beautiful and intricate patterns, which are painted in gay colors. This precious book is also in the British Museum.

Facing page 114—When the Bible was first legally permitted to be translated into English, every church was ordered to place an English Bible where anyone could read it. These Bibles were so precious that they were chained to the reading desk, as this one, from Lingfield in Surrey, still is.

Facing page 127—One of the treasures discovered on the site of the ancient city of Ur, in the valley of the Euphrates. It was found in a royal tomb and represents a ram caught in a thicket, made of wood covered with gold. It is 19½ inches high and was made about 2,500 B.C. Ur was, by tradition, the home of Abraham.

Facing page 129—A picture from an early English Bible, dating from the second quarter of the eleventh century. The boy Isaac is being taken by his father, Abraham, to be sacrificed as the Lord had commanded. The picture shows the journey, the ram caught in a thicket and the Lord stopping Abraham just in time. The story can be found in Genesis, chapter 22, verses 1-13.

INDEX